The Future of the Arab Spring

The Future of the Arab Spring

Civic Entrepreneurship in Politics, Art, and Technology Startups

Maryam Jamshidi

ELSEVIER

AMSTERDAM • BOSTON • HEIDELBERG • LONDON
NEW YORK • OXFORD • PARIS • SAN DIEGO
SAN FRANCISCO • SINGAPORE • SYDNEY • TOKYO
Butterworth-Heinemann is an imprint of Elsevier

Butterworth-Heinemann is an imprint of Elsevier
The Boulevard, Langford Lane, Kidlington, Oxford OX5 1GB, UK
225 Wyman Street, Waltham, MA 02451, USA

Notice
No responsibility is assumed by the publisher for any injury and/or damage to persons
or property as a matter of products liability, negligence or otherwise, or from any use or
operation of any methods, products, instructions or ideas contained in the material herein.
Because of rapid advances in the medical sciences, in particular, independent verification
of diagnoses and drug dosages should be made.

Library of Congress Cataloging-in-Publication Data
A catalogue record for this book is available from the Library of Congress.

British Library Cataloguing-in-Publication Data
A catalogue record for this book is available from the British Library.

ISBN: 978-0-12-416560-1

For information on all Butterworth-Heinemann publications
visit our website at store.elsevier.com

This book has been manufactured using Print On Demand technology. Each copy is
produced to order and is limited to black ink. The online version of this book will
show color figures where appropriate.

CONTENTS

To view photos, videos, and other supplemental material for this book, please visit: http://muftah.org/the-future-of-the-arab-spring-civic-entrepreneurship-in-politics-art-and-technology-startups/.

ACKNOWLEDGMENTS

It takes a village to write a book.

My heartfelt thanks go to the dozens of individuals who took time out of their busy schedules to speak to me about the various groups featured in this volume. I am indebted to the friends and colleagues who helped connect me to many of these groups or who suggested additional organizations I should profile. I am grateful to my close friends and family for bearing with me as I immersed myself in researching and writing and for their patience with my reclusive tendencies during this time. To my editor, Pam Chester, this book would not have been possible without your willingness to take a chance on a first-time writer. To my editorial project managers, Amber Hodge and Marisa LaFleur, thank you so much for going above and beyond the call of duty in working on this publication. Finally, a special thank you goes to EZ, who has helped make this and so many other dreams of mine a reality.

It goes without saying that any errors or mistakes in this volume are mine alone.

Maryam Jamshidi

CHAPTER *1*

Introduction

The revolutions of the Arab Spring,[1] which began in December 2010, mobilized millions of individuals across the Middle East and North Africa (MENA) to topple once untouchable autocratic leaders. As these events continue to impact countries in the MENA region, many are struggling to understand their long-term effects — is a new and better chapter being written in the Arab world or is this no more than a temporary break with the region's authoritarian past?

To assess the "success" of the Arab Spring, some have looked to indicators that traditionally define a country's health and well-being, including political and socio-economic markers. As a result, in the years since the revolutions began, focus has been placed on the various economic crises, the rise of Islamist parties, increases in sectarianism, and other challenges, both real and perceived, that have plagued numerous countries in the wake of the Arab Spring.

While these problems must be acknowledged, it is critical to rethink how we conceptualize and discuss the recent spate of uprisings in order to fully understand and appreciate the Arab Spring's achievements, as well as the challenges ahead. A new approach is needed — one that looks at the explosive rise in innovative groups, movements, organizations, startups, and other initiatives created by individuals at the grassroots levels to address various political, social, economic, and cultural issues in countries that have been rocked by the Arab Spring.

Since the revolutions began, there has been a stark increase in such groups and organizations, which signals an important paradigm shift. While shaped by different circumstances, these new initiatives highlight a critical transformation occurring in Arab Spring states — namely, the rise of civic entrepreneurism. Although commonly used to describe a particular kind of economic activity, as used here, civic entrepreneurship is

---

[1]The term "Arab Spring" is one among many phrases commonly used to describe recent events in the Arab world. Like many of these shorthand descriptions, its use is not without controversy. It is employed here, nevertheless, for simplicity's sake.

defined as any citizen-driven effort to mobilize communities to respond to opportunities or crises in order to advance the collective good.

Since the start of the Arab Spring, civic entrepreneurship has included the rise of protest movements and yielded innovative approaches to political mobilization and popular resistance, which have taken ruling regimes by surprise. It has spurred the creation of new groups and associations working to tackle local issues and build civic participation in regional countries. It has even encompassed an increasing number of technology startups led by young, educated individuals looking to solve everyday problems. Through these entities, activists, entrepreneurs, artists, musicians, filmmakers, and others have applied their talents to the task of rebuilding their countries' political, economic, social, and cultural fabric, in both direct and indirect ways. While emerging from the grassroots, these initiatives have, at times, had national and even regional consequences.

In countries impacted by the Arab Spring, civic entrepreneurism also reflects several new and important trends, including increased political and social awareness, a growing interest in collaborating with others on matters of common concern, a burgeoning commitment to self-expression and risk-taking, and a rejection of traditional social expectations, the politics of fear, and government intimidation. Collectively, these trends have profoundly shaped people's behaviors, hopes, and dreams in ways that are equally as important as the outcome of parliamentary elections and the health of national economies. Both in the short and long term, they have made the Arab Spring a truly unique and unprecedented phenomenon.

Although the development of civic entrepreneurship has not been analyzed on a national or regional level, it is critical to understanding the earliest days of the Arab Spring, as well as its future. For too long, stories of these generally uncoordinated grassroots developments have flown under the radar, largely viewed as disconnected anecdotes without broader significance. It is time to bring these stories into full focus and to appreciate what they demand: a reassessment of the nature of the Arab Spring, and a reformulation of how we understand concepts like revolution, ideology, and democracy.

Beyond its theoretical import, civic entrepreneurship represents a powerful shield and important weapon for protecting and defending the region's recent gains. As people in the Arab world have long since learned, governments promising change, reform, and improved standards of living cannot be wholly trusted to deliver on their commitments. The grassroots groups, organizations, and movements emerging from the region are the most important ingredients for holding these governments accountable and ensuring that revolutionary promises take root in Arab Spring societies over the long-term.

This book is intended to ignite conversations about the meaning, import, and practical significance of civic entrepreneurship during the Arab Spring by profiling some of the region's most inspiring groups, organizations, movements, and technology startups. Most of these entities emerged directly from the Arab world's incredible journey over the last several years, although some pre-existed but were radically transformed by the Arab Spring.

While initiatives like those featured here have arisen in a number of regional countries, the organizations profiled in this book draw predominately from the six states at the forefront of the Arab Spring: Tunisia, Egypt, Libya, Yemen, Bahrain, and Syria. This focus is not meant to diminish the importance of similar groups in other regional countries, but rather to encourage further study and examination of the growing trend in civic entrepreneurship throughout the Arab world since the start of the region's revolutions.

Similarly, in discussing these peaceful, innovative, and grassroots developments, there is no intention to minimize or gloss over the violence and physical insecurity that has and continues to exist in a number of Arab Spring states. Instead, the aim is to emphasize the revolutions' nonviolent roots, and to underscore the real and painful price many individuals in the Arab world have paid for engaging in collective acts of civil disobedience. For those regional countries riddled by armed conflict, it is these peaceful, collective, popular initiatives that hold the promise of a better future, if and when the fighting ends.

The profiles presented in the following chapters are based primarily on first-hand interviews with individual members or founders of these various entities, as well as on secondary sources. They are divided into three sections: Civic Entrepreneurship in Politics and Society, Civic Entrepreneurship in Art and Culture, and Civic Entrepreneurship in Technology Startups. Generally, these chapters discuss the founding and/or transformation of these groups, their evolution over the last several years, the kind of impact they aim to have, and the broader political, social, or economic landscape in which they exist.

But, first, to give context to this discussion, a look at the historical and theoretical issues that have and continue to shape the Arab Spring is in order. In this vein, Chapter Two provides a short history on the region in the decades preceding the Arab Spring, as well as a timeline of events for the revolutions in Tunisia, Egypt, Libya, Yemen, Bahrain, and Syria, which are relevant to the rest of this book. Chapter Three explores how the Arab Spring has redefined prevailing notions of revolution, ideology, and democracy, and how this relates to the rise of civic entrepreneurship in the region.

To view photos, videos, and other supplemental material for this book, please visit: http://muftah.org/the-future-of-the-arab-spring-civic-entrepreneurship-in-politics-art-and-technology-startups/

CHAPTER 2

A Short History of the Arab World and the Arab Spring

In order to understand where the Arab world is headed, it is critical to know where it has been.

During the last several decades, a never-ending cycle of autocracy, oppression, corruption, and economic stagnation gripped most MENA countries. Across the region, states were dominated by decades-long dictatorships that quashed freedoms of speech and expression, restricted opportunities to assemble and gather, committed egregious human rights abuses, and left domestic populations with little hope of social, professional, or economic mobility.

Some regional governments were styled as republics, born in the days of a long-since abandoned Arab nationalism, which had nominally combined transnational Arab unity with socialist principles. Other countries held true to monarchical traditions and were ruled by royal families of varied duration and provenance. Despite these differences in governance styles, many regional regimes maintained a tight grip on the political arena, and only allowed members of the ruling elite, government cronies, and the occasional technocrat to enjoy any semblance of political power.

Typically, these closed political systems combined with stagnant and undiversified economies, which were overly reliant on oil revenues. From the mid-twentieth century onwards, oil either directly or indirectly dominated the economic strategies of nearly all Arab states. In many oil-producing countries, income from oil sales made up the lion's share of GDP. In non oil-producing states, national economies often depended on remittances sent by young men who had moved to the Gulf's oil-rich countries in search of better job opportunities.

Because of these circumstances, the health of many Arab economies was intimately tied to volatile international oil markets. A number of regional governments were also saddled with substantial debt, in some cases due to profligate spending on military equipment supplied by the

United States. Repaying these loans grew increasingly challenging after international currency controls were abandoned in 1980 and oil prices began to drop in the mid-80s and throughout the 1990s. As a result, many Arab countries were thrown into economic crisis.

In a desperate attempt to save their national economies, some regional states turned to the International Monetary Fund (IMF) for loan relief. This set off a wave of neo-liberal economic policies, which recalibrated the social contract between states and citizens across the Arab world. The IMF's structural adjustment programs, which were attached as conditions to IMF and World Bank loans, dismantled many government-run industries and state-financed social services programs, which had been established during the 1950s and 60s. State-owned companies from Egypt to Jordan were privatized or shut down and subsidies on food and fuel were substantially cut.

Resulting increases in the cost of basic goods led to a number of "bread riots" across the Arab world beginning in the early 1980s. Governments in the MENA region had relied on food and energy subsidies to keep local populations complacent toward authoritarian state practices. By removing and/or substantially decreasing these social goods, many governments further undermined their credibility.

As neoliberalization programs swept through the region, public officials and government insiders took advantage of these policies to pocket kickbacks or purchase state-owed companies at cut-rate prices. In these ways, national wealth was transformed into private abundance for those with the money or connections to exploit deregulated economies. As ordinary citizens saw their incomes contract, the gap between the rich and poor in many Arab countries reached unprecedented levels. These problems did little to improve perceptions about the legitimacy of regional governments. By 2010, a study by Transparency International found that domestic populations in the vast majority of surveyed Arab countries perceived their governments to be more than moderately corrupt.[1]

Across many Arab countries, the ever-expanding size of national populations aggravated these various crises. In 1990, the MENA

---

[1]Corruption Perceptions Index 2010, Transparency International, http://www.transparency.org/cpi2010/results.

region's total population stood at 225.4 million.[2] By 2011, it had increased to 336.5 million.[3] Individuals between the ages of fifteen and twenty-four made up an increasingly large portion of this figure, reaching nearly 90 million by 2010.[4]

While literacy and education levels among this youth cohort were high, job opportunities lagged woefully behind. In a region where governments had long served as primary employers, neoliberal policies had substantially diminished public sector employment opportunities. To add insult to injury, those positions that were available were often subject to patronage practices. While many looked to the private sector as a solution to these problems, in most countries, private business was ill-equipped to absorb the large number of people entering the job market every year.

For many regional states, unemployment, especially among young people, remained a largely unaddressed and increasing problem throughout the 2000s. In 2009, the unemployment rate among youth in the MENA region reached 23.5%, the highest level of youth unemployment in the world at the time.[5] Against this backdrop, the region's informal economy, which typically provided low-paying jobs and was unregulated and untaxed, grew even further. Desperate to generate an income, large numbers of well-educated individuals entered this sector and took on work for which they were overqualified. Because of the dire economic situation, "delayed adulthood" became a common phenomenon among young people, with many postponing marriage until they had saved enough money to leave their parents' homes.

Despite the appalling political and economic conditions in many regional countries, Western governments were only too happy to keep these autocratic regimes in power. In both words and actions, the United States and its European friends implicitly agreed to politically and financially support many Arab dictatorships in exchange for a variety of commitments. These included the steady and guaranteed

---

[2] Poverty & Equity Data: Middle East and North Africa, The World Bank, http://povertydata.worldbank.org/poverty/region/MNA.

[3] Ibid.

[4] Farzaneh Roudi, "Youth Population and Employment in the Middle East and North Africa: Opportunity or Challenge?" United Nations Expert Group Meeting on Adolescents, Youth and Development, UN/POP/EGM-AYD/2011/06, June 22, 2011, http://www.un.org/esa/population/meetings/egm-adolescents/p06_roudi.pdf.

[5] Roudi, "Youth Population and Employment."

flow of oil, and support for Western, and particularly American, policies.[6] As long as Arab regimes followed through with this quid pro quo, the United States and European countries were only too willing to turn a blind eye to human rights violations, including state practices of torture and administrative detentions, as well as rampant government corruption.

2.1 THE ARAB SPRING ERUPTS

Despite this brewing storm of political, economic, and social problems, few people saw the Arab Spring coming.

2.1.1 Tunisia

Things began quietly on December 17, 2010, when Mohamed Bouazizi, a twenty-six-year old Tunisian fruit seller from the impoverished city of Sidi Bouzid, set himself on fire. Like many young people in the region, Bouazizi had received a university education, but was forced into the informal jobs sector after failing to find proper employment.

As the young man was beginning his day on the 17th, a policewoman attempted to confiscate his fruit cart. When Bouazizi resisted, the woman slapped him and yelled various insults. Embarrassed by the public humiliation, the young man headed to the local municipality building and set himself on fire. In anger over his death, Bouazizi's friends took to the streets, in what would become the first in a series of demonstrations inside Tunisia.

In very literal fashion, Bouazizi's death lit a spark inside the country, unleashing decades of frustration toward an autocratic, corrupt, and bloated regime. Protests quickly spread from Sidi Bouzid to other parts of Tunisia, and soon reached the capital, Tunis. Rampant unemployment was a particular focus of the peaceful insurrection with a variety of protests organized around a call for jobs.

[6]Many of the West's regional policies also served the repressive interests of Arab autocracies. As Islamist groups became increasingly popular in various regional countries, many Arab regimes oppressed or significantly curtailed their activities, often arresting or exiling prominent Islamist leaders. For these governments, supporting the U.S. War on Terror was hardly a stretch. In fact, both before and after September 11, the West's Arab allies frequently exaggerated the threat from Islamist groups, both to ensure continuing Western support and to justify illiberal policies to domestic audiences.

Throughout late December/early January, protests continued, crossing socio economic lines and drawing in lawyers, students, and other activists. The government responded violently, using tear gas against protesters and even beating and shooting unarmed demonstrators. Only a few weeks after the uprising began, on January 14, 2011, Tunisian President Zine el Abidine Ben Ali was ousted from power after twenty-three years in office.

2.1.2 Egypt

Inspired by the rapid success of the Tunisian mobilization, an informal network of Egyptian activists scheduled their own demonstrations for the "National Police Day" holiday[7] on January 25, 2011. Across a variety of cities, the January 25 demonstrations attracted more participants than expected, with thousands filling Egypt's streets.

As in Tunisia, events moved quickly and unexpectedly. While the protests began with calls for government reform, demands for President Hosni Mubarak's ouster quickly became more common. On January 28, Mubarak ordered Egyptian troops onto the streets, dismissed his cabinet, and refused popular calls to step down. On January 29, the President appointed Omar Sulieman, the country's notorious intelligence chief, to the post of vice president, a position that had been virtually eliminated during the Mubarak regime.

On February 1, 2011, approximately one million people poured onto the streets, including 200,000 in Cairo, demanding Mubarak step down after nearly thirty-one years in power. That same day, Mubarak gave a televised speech, promising constitutional amendments and vowing not to run in upcoming presidential elections. His comments resonated and moved many Egyptians, who considered abandoning the protests on the strength of his promised reforms.

Only a day later, on February 2, this goodwill disappeared after pro-Mubarak supporters riding horses and camels and armed with various weapons attacked largely peaceful protesters in Tahrir Square. The infamous clashes, which came to be known as the "Battle of the

---

[7]Declared an official national holiday in 2009, Egypt's Police Day commemorated the death of fifty Egyptian police officers at the hands of the British army on January 25, 1952. Because the 2011 demonstrations were intended in part to highlight police abuse, activists chose this day for its symbolic value.

Camel," shifted momentum in favor of the protest movement. Egypt had crossed the Rubicon.

On February 9, the country's labor unions joined the protests, raising concerns about the crippling effect on the economy and ending any lingering hopes the regime could emerge intact from the uprising. On February 11, eighteen days after protests began, Mubarak was ousted from power.

For all those skeptical about the course of events in the region, it was hard to deny that something important was afoot.

2.1.3 Libya

In Libya, protests began on February 15, 2011, with several hundred demonstrators gathering in front of police headquarters in Benghazi, the country's second largest city, to challenge the arrest of human rights activist, Fathi Terbil. Things took a dramatic turn only a few days later when thousands of Libyans took to the streets on February 17 in a "day of rage" modeled after the region's other uprisings.

Unlike Egypt and Tunisia, protests in Libya quickly escalated into violent confrontations between government factions and forces opposed to Libyan leader Muammar Ghaddafi. On February 20, anti-Ghaddafi fighters seized Benghazi after fighting regime forces for days and capturing several other towns in eastern Libya. The government struck back, shelling various cities and towns in the eastern region.

On February 26, the United Nations Security Council passed Resolution 1970, condemning Ghaddafi's use of lethal force against protesters, imposing a series of international sanctions against various Libyan officials and members of the Ghaddafi family, instituting an arms embargo, and referring Libya to the International Criminal Court (ICC) for crimes allegedly committed since the start of the protests. On March 5, the National Transitional Council (NTC), Libya's official opposition body, formed in Benghazi and took charge of organizing the uprising.

Less than a month after the ICC referral, the Security Council authorized a no-fly zone in Libya, purportedly to protect civilian populations against government attack. Adopted on March 17, Resolution 1973 also "[a]uthoriz[ed] Member States that have notified the Secretary-General, acting nationally or through regional organizations or arrangements, and acting in cooperation with the Secretary-General, to take all necessary measures to protect civilians and civilian populated areas under threat of attack in the Libyan Arab Jamahiriya."[8]

Only days after the resolution's passage, on March 19, the United States, Britain, and France launched an air strike over Libya against the regime. On March 31, the North Atlantic Treaty Organization (NATO) assumed responsibility for military operations in the country, pursuant to Resolutions 1973 and 1970. Although authorized only to protect civilians, in August 2011, NATO provided direct air support for a number of NTC operations, including its first attack on Tripoli, the Libyan capital.

On September 21, NATO officials agreed to extend the Libyan mission for up to ninety days. On October 20, NATO forces supported NTC fighters in their final assault on the city of Sirte, which ended with Ghaddafi's death. After forty-three years in power, the regime of Muammar Ghaddafi had come to an end. The NATO mission to Libya officially concluded on October 31, 2011.

2.1.4 Yemen

Yemen's revolution began with a small demonstration on January 16, 2011, when less than thirty protesters gathered in front of Sana'a University to call for President Ali Abdullah Saleh's resignation. The protest was led by activist and future Nobel Peace Prize winner Tawakul Karman. Karman was arrested only a few days later on January 22, leading to further protests demanding her release.

Demonstrations continued to grow in size over the course of February, with protesters calling for Saleh's resignation, economic reforms, and an end to corruption. On February 2, Saleh vowed that neither he nor his son would run in elections scheduled for 2013.[9] The move had little impact, as people headed to the streets only a day later to once again call for Saleh's overthrow. By early March, demonstrations in Yemen topped one million protesters.

---

[8]United Nations Security Council, Res. 1973, par. 4, S/Res/1973, March 17, 2011, http://www.un
.org/ga/search/view_doc.asp?symbol=S/RES/1973(2011).
[9]It was widely believed that Saleh had been grooming his eldest son, Ahmed, for the presidency.

With protests showing no signs of slowing down, in April Saleh agreed to allow the Gulf Cooperation Council (GCC) to open negotiations with opposition forces to end the crisis.[10] By this point, protests had already become deadly, with government forces taking lethal action against demonstrators on a number of occasions.[11] On June 3, the presidential palace in the capital of Sana'a was attacked, leading to several deaths and resulting in Saleh's injury. Soon after the incident, Yemen's vice president, Abdu Rabbu Mansour Hadi, was named acting president while Saleh traveled to Saudi Arabia to receive treatment for his injuries.

After backing out of negotiations several times, in November 2011, Saleh finally accepted a GCC-brokered deal to step down from office after thirty-three years in power. In accordance with the agreement, presidential elections were held in February 2012, bringing Hadi to office.[12]

2.1.5 Bahrain

In Bahrain, nationwide protests were called for February 14, 2011, to mark the tenth anniversary of a constitutional referendum that had failed to bring promised reforms to the country.[13] As people took to the streets that day, they were greeted by violence. Security personnel dispersed gathered crowds, arrested a number of participants, and killed one demonstrator. Undeterred, Bahrainis held more demonstrations the next day. Taking a chapter from Egypt's revolution, protesters occupied the Pearl Roundabout, the central traffic circle in Manama, the country's capital.

---

[10]The GCC is a political and economic union of Arab states bordering the Persian Gulf and includes Bahrain, Kuwait, Oman, Qatar, Saudi Arabia, and the UAE.

[11]The "Friday of Dignity" massacre was among the most devastating acts of government violence. The incident took place in Sana'a on March 18, on the edge of Change Square, the center of Yemen's then-growing protest movement. As tens of thousands of protesters ended their midday prayers, masked gunmen began shooting from the surrounding rooftops, trees, and streets. Two hundred people were injured and forty-five were killed. "Yemen: Massacre Investigation Badly Flawed," *Human Rights Watch*, September 27, 2012, http://www.hrw.org/news/2012/09/27/yemen-massacre-investigation-badly-flawed.

[12]Although Hadi was the only candidate on the ballot, voter turnout for the presidential elections was relatively high.

[13]Bahrain's National Action Charter, which contained a series of political and social reforms, was approved in 2001 through a national referendum. While the charter brought about some political liberalization, many promised reforms remained a dead letter.

Although demonstrators came mostly from the country's beleaguered Shia community, they expressed grievances that focused not on religion but rather on political, economic, and social justice issues. Protesters called for a transition to a constitutional monarchy, the resignation of the prime minister, greater civil liberties, and the creation of a popularly elected parliament with real powers, among other demands.

Likely do to the cross-sectarian nature of its goals, the protest movement appealed to a wide swath of Bahrainis and quickly grew in size over the course of late February/early March. On February 25, protests swelled to approximately 200,000 participants, representing about forty percent of the indigenous Bahraini population.[14]

As the crisis intensified, the Al Khalifa monarchy, Bahrain's ruling regime, sought assistance from outside forces. On March 14, the GCC agreed to step in and deploy the Peninsula Shield Force, its military arm. That same day, security forces from Saudi Arabia and the UAE arrived to quash the country's demonstrations. On March 15, King Hamad bin Isa Al Khalifa declared a three-month state of emergency to help "restore order."[15] Only a few days later, on March 18, authorities destroyed the Pearl Roundabout, which had become the heart of the protest movement.

The violence, intimidation, and repression unleashed against Bahrain's peaceful protesters were particularly brutal and severe, even for the region. Wounded demonstrators were targeted at hospitals. Midnight house raids were regularly carried out in homes across various Shia neighborhoods. Countless civilians were stopped at checkpoints set up across the country, where they were abused and beaten. Hundreds of workers, who participated in the demonstrations, were dismissed from government jobs and positions in state-linked firms. Security officials arrested bloggers, cyber activists, and human rights advocates, as well as doctors and nurses who dared treat injured protesters. Many of those arrested were ultimately brought before military courts for trial and sentencing.

---

[14]Stephen Zunes, "America Blows It on Bahrain," *Foreign Policy in Focus*, March 2, 2011, http://www.fpif.org/articles/america_blows_it_on_bahrain.

[15]"Two Killed in Bahrain Violence Despite Martial Law," *BBC*, March 15, 2011, http://www.bbc.co.uk/news/world-middle-east-12751464.

As the state-sanctioned brutality continued, the Bahraini govern-ment made superficial overtures toward national reconciliation. In June 2011, the king ordered the creation of the Bahrain Independent Commission of Inquiry (BICI) to investigate alleged crimes committed in the early days of the uprising. The BICI issued its final report in November 2011, documenting a damning array of crimes committed by the Bahraini government. Despite promises to implement the BICI's recommended reforms, the regime has failed (as of this writing) to make substantial strides in overhauling problematic state practices or holding officials accountable for the abuse and death of protesters.

Despite these setbacks and challenges, Bahrain's protest movement, which now aims to oust the regime, continues in different forms. Amid continuing repression, activists have organized smaller demonstrations and engaged in other forms of grassroots mobilization and civil disobedience. Though the Al Khalifa regime remains in power, the opposition movement shows no signs of wavering in its commitment to toppling the government.

2.1.6 Syria

In Syria, nationwide protests emerged in mid-March 2011 after several boys between the ages of nine and fifteen were arrested in the rural city of Deraa in late February for spraying graffiti that read "[t]he peo-ple want to topple the regime."[16] Among other demands, demonstra-tors called for the release of all political prisoners, the abolition of Syria's nearly fifty-year emergency law, more freedoms, and an end to pervasive corruption.[17]

From the start, the Syrian regime reacted violently to the peaceful protests, using live ammunition against unarmed civilians. Government brutality only served to increase the size and frequency of demonstrations. After initially refusing to make any concessions, on April 3, President Bashar al-Assad dismissed his cabinet and appointed a new prime minister. A few days later, Assad promised greater politi-cal and social rights to the Syrian people, and, on April 21, issued a decree to end the country's emergency law. Peaceful protests contin-ued, however, as did the regime's brutality. By early May, the civilian

---

[16]While the slogan was a common one from the Arab uprisings, it was a dangerous show of defi-ance in the tightly controlled Syrian police state.

[17]The children, who had been beaten and tortured, were eventually released in late March.

death toll was estimated at over 1,100.[18] As events escalated, protesters eventually began calling for Assad's ouster.

The first instances of armed rebellion came in early June 2011 in the northern province of Idlib. In July, a video posted on YouTube announced the formation of the Free Syrian Army (FSA), which was composed of defectors from the Syrian Armed Forces as well as other volunteers.[19] The FSA, which has since become the opposition's main armed group, was specifically formed to remove Assad from power. In August 2011, the Syrian National Council (SNC) was founded. Made up of a coalition of different groups, the SNC aimed to coordinate opposition efforts against the regime. In December 2011, the SNC began working more closely with the FSA.

In November 2011, the Arab League officially suspended Syria's membership in the organization, while also imposing a series of sanctions against the regime. By December 2011, the death toll inside Syria had risen to over 5,000.[20] Although armed insurrection had become increasingly common, various forms of peaceful protest were still taking place. On December 30, 2011, an estimated 500,000 people participated in demonstrations around the country, the largest mass protest until that point.[21]

The regime was unwilling to tolerate any form of dissent. As peaceful demonstrations continued, the government rounded up tens of thousands of people, with a focus on nonviolent activists, as well as boys and men from towns the Syrian Army had besieged or retaken from the armed opposition. These mass crackdowns helped fuel more violence, inspiring some individuals to take up arms. Unsurprisingly, between the latter-half of 2011 and mid-2012, a full-scale, widespread, armed opposition movement began to overtake Syria's peaceful protests.

Echoing similar calls from leaders in the United States, United Kingdom, Germany, and other nations, the UN General Assembly passed a non-binding resolution on February 16, 2012, urging the

[18]"Conflict Timeline," *Syria Deeply*, http://beta.syriadeeply.org/conflict-timeline/.
[19]"The Formation of the Free Syrian Army," YouTube, July 29, 2011, http://www.youtube.com/watch?feature=player_embedded&v=SZcCbIPM37w.
[20]"Conflict Timeline," *Syria Deeply*.
[21]Ibid.

Syrian president to leave office. Various UN envoys were also sent to the country to broker a cease-fire and a permanent cessation of hostilities, but to no avail.

Amid continued fighting between regime and opposition forces, the National Coalition for Syrian Revolutionary and Opposition Forces was founded in November 2012. The Syrian National Coalition, as the group is commonly known, united the SNC with several other opposition groups under one umbrella organization. By March 2013, the coalition had officially obtained formal recognition as the legitimate government of Syria from the United States, France, Britain, the Arab League, and over a 100 other countries.

In February 2013, UN High Commissioner for Human Rights, Navi Pillay, speculated that the death toll in Syria is "probably now approaching 70,000."[22] As of this writing, the armed conflict continues.

While events in Tunisia, Egypt, Libya, Yemen, Bahrain, and Syria have dominated the headlines, demonstrations also broke out in other regional countries, including Jordan, Morocco, Sudan, and Saudi Arabia. While many of these protests have continued to take place at varying rates of frequency and size, they have yet to reach the critical mass witnessed in these other Arab Spring countries.

2.1.7 Euphoria Turns Sour

During the early days of the Arab Spring, a euphoric wave overtook the region. After decades of economic, social, and political deterioration, people in the Arab world had rediscovered the power of their own voices and the force of their collective will. Not since the days of pan-Arab nationalism had populations in various regional countries been united by such a sense of transnational hope and optimism about the future. Events in the region were also an example to the rest of the world. Indeed, even in the United States, the Arab Spring's reverberations could be felt.[23]

---

[22]Michelle Nichols, "Syria Death Toll Likely Near 70,000, Says UN Rights Chief," *Reuters*, February 12, 2013, http://www.reuters.com/article/2013/02/12/us-syria-crisis-un-idUSBRE91B19C20130212.

[23]The Occupy Wall Street movement, which was established in September 2011 to advocate for political, social, and economic justice in the United States, was organized by activists consciously influenced by the uprisings in the Arab world.

But, as euphoria is wont to do, feelings of giddy optimism about the Arab Spring started to dissipate. As a number of regional uprisings appeared to fizzle out or turn violent, anxiety and concern developed about the Arab Spring's trajectory. For numerous individuals inside and outside the region, growing doubts emerged as to whether the revolutions were capable of permanently changing the status quo. Some began to critique the lack of cohesive planning or strategy behind these events. Who or what would replace deposed leaders? What were the revolutions' specific demands, and how would they be achieved? What steps would be taken to institutionalize political changes, particularly in the face of strong counter-revolutionary trends?

These criticisms were leveled not only against the Arab Spring's more questionable "successes," but also against those revolutions that had managed to oust authoritarian rulers. In the words of Middle East expert, Asef Bayat, "Two years after the fall of the dictators in Tunisia, Egypt and Yemen not a great deal has effectively changed in the states' institutions or the power bases of the old elites. Police, army and judiciary; state-controlled media; business elites and the clientelist networks of the old ruling parties – all remained more or less intact."[24]

In Tunisia, divisions between secularists and Islamists emerged both socially and politically soon after Ben Ali's ouster. While free and fair parliamentary elections were successfully held in October 2011, the victory of long oppressed Islamist party, Ennahda,[25] did little to calm tensions or diffuse the country's growing political and economic problems. Since taking the reins of government, Ennahda has struggled to solidify its hold on power, been embroiled in various controversies, and received serious criticism about its efforts to steer the country through numerous crises. Tunisia's economic situation also continues to deteriorate, with rising inflation and unemployment levels.

[24]Asef Bayat, "Revolution in Bad Times," *New Left Review*, vol. 8, March-April 2013, http://newleftreview.org/II/80/asef-bayat-revolution-in-bad-times.

[25]Ennahda was founded in Tunisia in 1981 and quickly grew to become an influential force within the country. While initially shaped by more violent, extremist writings, Ennahda evolved in the 1980s to become a more moderate Islamist group, supporting democracy and political pluralism. Because of the group's growing influence, the Tunisian government began to repress Ennahda in the late 1980s. The party was banned from participating in parliamentary elections in 1989 and, in 1991, 25,000 Ennahda members were imprisoned by the Ben Ali regime. From 1992 until the Tunisian revolution, Ennahda was virtually absent from the country's limited public sphere, with most of its leaders either in jail or in exile.

In Egypt, Mubarak's ouster was just the beginning of a protracted economic, social, and political crisis. To guide the country's transition until presidential and parliamentary elections could be held, the Supreme Council of the Armed Forces (SCAF), an unelected military body composed of top Mubarak-era army officers, was immediately installed upon the president's departure. While the military has long-enjoyed broad popularity among Egyptians, during its sixteen-month rule, SCAF used its executive authority to behave more like a military dictatorship than a benevolent caretaker government – its tenure was characterized by efforts to grant itself sweeping powers, remove the military, and its budget, from civilian oversight, enforce martial law in the country, arrest and detain protesters and activists, and postpone parliamentary elections.

In June 2012, Egypt successfully held free and fair presidential elections that formally brought the SCAF regime to a close.[26] The victory of Mohamed Morsi, the Muslim Brotherhood's[27] candidate, did little, however, to alter the many political, social, and economic challenges facing Egypt's transitional process.

While in office, Morsi failed to endear himself to many segments of the Egyptian population, including liberals, nationalists, revolutionary youth, and various minority groups. Among other missteps, the president issued a decree in November 2012 that appeared on its face (if not in its ultimate application) to bolster his authority.[28] Shortly thereafter, Morsi rammed through a new constitution that various

---

[26]While SCAF's direct rule over the country may have ended, the military still exerted considerable influence from behind the scenes, as it had always done.

[27]Founded in Egypt in 1928 by a schoolteacher named Hasan al-Banna, the Muslim Brotherhood has become one of the most influential Islamist organizations in the country as well as the broader Middle East. From its beginnings, the Brotherhood functioned as a hybrid organization that married ideology with action, combining Islamic principles with an abiding sense of social justice. To help the poor and other needy individuals, the Brotherhood historically provided religious education as well as a broad array of social services. These efforts helped increase the group's popularity in various countries where it operated. This popularity also earned the organization some powerful enemies among regional authoritarian regimes. In Egypt, the Brotherhood was banned for most of its existence, a situation that only changed after Mubarak's ouster. For more on the Muslim Brotherhood, see Nancy J. Davis and Robert V. Robinson, *Claiming Society for God: Religious Movements and Social Welfare* (Bloomington: Indiana University Press, 2012), 32-60.

[28]Among its various provisions, the decree immunized the president's actions from judicial review. In response to mass protests, Morsi rescinded this and a number of other articles contained in the decree only a few weeks later, in early December 2012.

non-Islamist groups objected to on procedural and substantive grounds.[29] He also failed to institute many of the revolution's demands, including reforming Egypt's hated security sector. Instead, the president stood by as an increasing number of high-profile media personalities and activists were brought in for questioning by government officials. Under Morsi's stewardship, the country's economic situation also reached a crisis point, with sovereign debt levels soaring to near-unprecedented levels, increasing unemployment, and slow rates of economic growth.

Meanwhile, Egypt's opposition groups, including the April 6 Youth Movement, a political organization formed in 2008, and the National Salvation Front (NSF), an umbrella group of liberals, socialists, nationalists, and others, failed to develop coherent political platforms that resonated with a broad spectrum of the Egyptian public. Against this backdrop, some Egyptians, unhappy with prevailing circumstances in the country, started to agitate for military intervention.

In early May 2013, a group of young activists organized a signature campaign called Tamarrod, or "Rebellion," calling for Morsi to step aside as president and demanding early elections. On June 30, Tamarrod-sponsored demonstrations brought millions onto Egypt's streets. As protests continued, on July 1, the army formally intervened and gave the president forty-eight hours to resolve the stand off. On July 3, the military, with the backing of millions of demonstrators, as well as a coalition of liberals, revolutionaries, and Salafist[30] groups, ousted Morsi from power and suspended the new constitution. An interim government was selected to rule the country, until parliamentary and presidential elections could be held.

---

[29]The debate about Egypt's constitution is complex and beyond the scope of this book. In short, many who objected to the document argued it was created by a non-representative Constituent Assembly dominated by Islamists. Although the assembly did have a number of non-Islamist members, detractors insist these individuals were unable to make meaningful contributions to the drafting process. Most experts agree, however, that the final draft was, at worst, mediocre, and did not represent an attempt to entrench the Brotherhood or Islamism in Egyptian politics. For more on Egypt's constitutional drafting process see "Arab Uprising: The Battle for Egypt's Constitution," Project on Middle East Political Science, January 11, 2013, http://pomeps.org/wp-content/uploads/2013/01/POMEPS_BriefBooklet17_Egypt_web.pdf.

[30]Salafism is a branch of Sunni Islam that embraces a literalist, and some would say puritanical, interpretation of Islamic scripture. Salafism venerates the earliest descendants of the first Muslim community and presents them as examples for all subsequent generations to follow.

In Libya, the revolution ended the cult of Ghaddafi, which for decades had made the state synonymous with the former leader. Despite security challenges in some parts of the country, credible, multiparty parliamentary elections were successfully held in July 2012, bringing a mixture of liberals, Brotherhood members, Salafists, and independent candidates to office.

The end of the Ghaddafi regime coupled with months of armed conflict also brought a number of unelected political players to power. In a country where local and tribal allegiances have historically been important, these parochial groups have gained increased influence and continue to vie for control over important public and private assets, including the state security sector, national expenditures, and valuable smuggling routes.

Many militia groups, established during and after the military conflict, are still heavily armed. Refusing to be disbanded, they have flexed their muscles to maintain influence in the country. Most of these groups have pursued decidedly local goals, connected to family, tribe, or town. Because of these circumstances, cities that were centers of revolutionary activity during the conflict have become local power centers in post-war Libya.

Against this backdrop, the central government remains relatively weak, particularly with regard to security issues. Groups and tribes with historical grievances have used this power vacuum to settle scores. Ghaddafi-era intelligence officers have been particular victims of these extrajudicial actions, as a significant number of these former officials have been murdered since the end of the war. Amid these and other challenges, the transition to a new Libya remains a decidedly unfinished project.

In Yemen, change has been similarly slow in coming, with many placing blame on the GCC agreement. For a number of activists and observers, this deal represents little more than an attempt to sideline the revolution, preserve the status quo, and ensure that Yemen's uprising does not spill over into neighboring countries, like Saudi Arabia. While the GCC agreement called for various reforms, it did not ban Saleh or his family from participating in the country's political and military spheres. Indeed, Saleh, who resides in the country, still wields substantial influence over Yemeni politics and heads up the General

People's Congress, the country's former ruling party. Members of Saleh's family also continue to hold important positions within the military and government. Their continued involvement in Yemen's affairs has been a substantial barrier to instituting meaningful change in the country.

U.S. drone attacks have substantially increased since President Hadi's election, creating popular outrage against the U.S. and Yemeni governments, and further destabilizing the country. Yemen's humanitarian crisis, which began before the revolution, has also continued and increased in severity. It is little surprise, then, that for many in the country the revolutionary struggle continues despite Saleh's resignation.

On top of these troubling developments across various Arab Spring states, some actors inside and outside the MENA region viewed the rise of "Islamist" governments as an unmitigated disaster. From the revolutions' earliest days, these individuals and entities cringed at the possibility that Islamist groups, such as the Brotherhood, would come to power in Arab countries rocked by upheaval.

Indeed, even before elections were held, the victory of these organizations was all but assured. Most Islamist groups outlawed by predecessor governments were untainted by the crimes and corruption of these regimes. Instead, years of political repression had given these organizations a veneer of credibility, which was further strengthened by their work in providing social services governments could not or would not provide.

In an environment of free and fair elections, Islamist groups were sure to skate to an easy victory, especially in the short term. Never mind that the Arab Spring had neither been started nor led by these organizations, some of which had initially hesitated to join the uprisings. Years of one-party rule in many Arab states had made these groups the only game in town. When elections in various Arab Spring countries brought Islamist organizations to power, those inherently inclined to see them in a negative light viewed these developments as a setback for the region.

Such prognostications were heard, in part, from Western voices upset by the loss of secular authoritarian allies in the Arab world. For these actors, Islamists were perceived to be more hostile to Western interests, unwilling to continue the pro-Israel policies of predecessor regimes, less inclined to allow natural resources to be exploited by Western firms, and more likely to oppose any collaboration or alliance with Western, particularly U.S. and Israeli, militaries. Liberals, secularists, and various other groups in the region were also less than enthusiastic about the rise of political Islam. Many of these groups distrusted the willingness of Islamists to respect human rights and pluralism and feared they would disregard democratic principles upon coming to power.

Whatever one may think about the accuracy of these particular apprehensions, there were other changes afoot — transformations that were taking place on the individual and grassroots levels, which spoke to the Arab Spring's positive impact in many regional countries.

CHAPTER 3

Revolution, Ideology, and Democracy

While some Western and regional commentators have raised alarm bells about Islamism, and as new governments have struggled to rule Arab Spring countries dominated by bloated bureaucracies and broken economies, individual citizens have been busy transforming their communities and addressing local and national problems through grassroots organizations, movements, startups, and other forms of civic entrepreneurship.

To appreciate how and why these entrepreneurial efforts have emerged, we must revisit mainstream understandings of revolution, ideology, and democracy as applied to the Arab Spring. Over the last several years, these approaches have been dominated by three trends: (1) an overly historicized depiction of "revolution;" (2) a definition of "ideology" that is limited to political, religious, or economic dogmas; and (3) a reading of "democracy" that relies primarily on the ballot box and excludes social justice issues.

This chapter examines why these trends fail to accurately capture the Arab Spring. Most importantly, it demonstrates how civic entrepreneurism challenges these approaches and reformulates the concepts of revolution, ideology, and democracy in ways that better reflect the nature of the region's uprisings.

3.1 REVOLUTION

From the Arab Spring's earliest days, one question has loomed large: should the protests sweeping across the region be defined as "revolutions"? More than a semantic or philosophical debate, these discussions have profoundly impacted perceptions about the Arab Spring's "success," influenced how that success is defined, and shaped expectations about the future of these uprisings.

While the literature on revolutionary studies is deep and complex, for our purposes, there are primarily two ways to understand and analyze revolutions — the first is through a theoretical lens and the second is through a historical one. While these approaches are not mutually exclusive, they privilege different strategies and often yield very different results.

The "theory of revolution" focuses on the concept's basic building blocks and evolution. It draws up general themes from a wide variety of revolutionary events, and charts the concept's development over time. In so doing, it provides a substantive guide for identifying "revolutions," while remaining adaptable. It appreciates that guidelines may shift in response to current events or new understandings of history and encourages reassessment where necessary. Under this approach, less emphasis is placed on a particular historical moment or the substance of concrete revolutionary demands, although these details can be informative.

By contrast, the "history of revolution" compares specific events in the present and past to determine what is and is not a revolution. Under this approach, current events are more likely to be considered "revolutionary" if they are similar to particular revolutions in history. Focus is typically placed on how events developed, the actors involved, the kinds of demands made, and other facts necessary to compare current happenings to particular historical moments. This method usually applies a more static notion of "revolution," although the definition may vary based on the specific historical event that frames the analysis.

It is this latter method that has largely dominated understandings of the Arab Spring. In the weeks, months, and years since these events began, many have looked for similarities between the region's uprisings and Eastern Europe's 1989 Velvet Revolutions, the Iranian revolution of 1979, and even the wave of European uprisings in 1848, among other historical moments.

Similarities between current events in the Arab world and these past revolutions have, however, been few and far between. Most of these earlier revolutions resulted in radical changes to pre-existing political systems, such as Iran's replacement of a secular monarchy with an Islamic theocracy. Many of these historical events also had identifiable leaders. For instance, by the time the Velvet Revolutions began, charismatic opposition figures had emerged in a variety of Eastern European countries, including Polish labor-rights organizer Lech Walesa, and the

Czech writer and playwright Vaclav Havel. By contrast, in most Arab Spring countries, recent events have yet to bring about large-scale political transformations or give rise to identifiable revolutionary leaders.

These and other differences have prompted some commentators to dismiss most of the Arab Spring uprisings as reformist at best and utter failures at worst. The theory of revolution pushes back on these conclusions, however. Urging reflection on the evolving nature of the concept, this approach emphasizes the fluidity and subjectivity of defining what is and is not a revolution.

As Fred Halliday, the noted political theorist, has observed, "[D]efinitions of revolution are, like all definitions in social sciences, conventional: revolutions are not − anymore than are nations, classes, even events or dates − objectively given 'things,' waiting to be unearthed or identified like the objects of natural science. They are phenomena which human subjects choose to group, on the basis of criteria of significance and recurrence, into one category rather than another."[1]

Under the theory of revolution, the following four "criteria of significance" have defined the concept in modern times: (1) popular involvement; (2) progress; (3) the start of a new age; and (4) total transformation. "Popular involvement" means exactly what the term suggests − the large-scale mobilization of a country's population. "Progress" is defined as the linear movement of history in a positive direction, so that revolutions represent net gains for impacted societies. A "new age" refers to "a break with the constraints of the past, the traditional or established society ... allow[ing] a new society, even a new world, to be constructed,"[2] while "total transformation" points not just to "a change in the political or constitutional form of society, but also a change in economic structure, in values and beliefs, and even in dress, language, and systems of calculating time."[3]

Events in many parts of the Arab world clearly satisfy the first two criteria of "popular involvement" and "progress." In Arab Spring countries, protest movements began at the grassroots level and enjoyed widespread popular support. While their demands were initially

---

[1]Fred Halliday, *Revolution and World Politics: the Rise and Fall of the Sixth Great Power* (Durham, N.C.: Duke University Press, 1999), 47.
[2]Ibid., 36.
[3]Ibid., 38.

dominated by vague requests for reform or general calls for the ouster of ruling regimes, in many cases, they developed concrete, issue-based platforms, which have been described as "progressive" and "forward-thinking" efforts at political, social, and economic change.

Although the Arab Spring may not neatly fit the remaining two criteria of a "new age" and "total transformation," regional events demand a reassessment of these terms, as permitted by the theory of revolution. While most Arab Spring countries have yet to institutionalize a new body politic, this does not mean change of some kind has not happened or that large-scale alterations will not eventually occur. Widespread calls for the ouster of ruling regimes at the start of the region's uprisings demonstrated a popular desire for transformative political change in many Arab Spring states. It is here, from among the people at the grassroots level, where a "new age" has continued to unfold and where "total transformations," in terms of individual expectations and actions, have been taking place since the revolutions' early days.

The spirit of civic entrepreneurism, reflected in the rise of new groups, organizations, startups, and projects that emerged from or have been impacted by the Arab Spring, underscores these realities and embodies new values, such as collaboration and collective action, which are transforming regional societies at the grassroots level.

This reassessment of revolution, based on the concepts of civic entrepreneurism and popular action, is, in fact, very much embedded in the revolutionary tradition. As noted political theorist Hannah Arendt has observed, all revolutions at their core revolve around taking action and starting something new, "[they represent the] determination to act, [the] joy in action, the assurance of being able to change things by one's own efforts."[4]

As the Arab Spring teaches us, while broad macro-level transformations are important, widespread changes taking place at the grassroots level substantially contribute to revolutionary alterations. In fact, grassroots transformations occurring in Arab Spring countries strongly suggest that the region's revolutions continue, and that a complete political, social, and economic overhaul is on the horizon.

[4]Hannah Arendt, "Thoughts on Politics and Revolution," in *Crises of the Republic* (New York: Harvest/HJB, 1972), 206.

As renowned cultural critic Hamid Dabashi has observed, "The longer [the Arab Spring] take[s] to unfold the more enduring, grass-roots based, and definitive will be [its] emotive, symbolic, and institutional consequences."[5]

Civic entrepreneurism reflects the continuing spirit of collective action and collaboration that defined the revolutions' early days and keeps these sentiments alive. This is where the momentum to bring about broader transformative change in regional states is currently being created and nurtured.

3.2 IDEOLOGY

While some have argued that the Arab Spring was "non-ideological," ideology has, in fact, been very much on display during the region's various revolutions. For all the negative and critical commentary about their exclusivist and socially destructive consequences, ideologies can also be useful tools that help societies evaluate and guide their actions.[6] The ideology of the Arab Spring serves these productive ends, while also defying traditional notions of the term.

Typically, ideology is understood as embracing specific economic, social, political, or religious programs. These kinds of ideologies have been an important part of many, if not most, modern revolutions. In some cases, these ideological discourses have provided the inspirational political philosophy behind revolutionary movements. In other cases, revolutions have expressly aimed to overthrow certain ideological programs. In still other cases, revolutionary activities have been fueled by factions with various and often conflicting ideological perspectives that have looked beyond their differences to unite around a common cause.

There is, however, another part of the ideological spectrum, which represents a manner of thinking more than a particular political, religious, or economic platform. This kind of ideology relates to shifting mind-sets, and distinguishes between pre-revolutionary and post-revolutionary worldviews. Centered more on form than substance, this

---

[5]Hamid Dabashi, *The Arab Spring: The End of Postcolonialism* (London: Zed Books, 2012), 6.

[6]Islamic scholar, Tariq Ramadan, describes the relationship between ideology and society as follows, "A human society without ideology is like an animal without instincts: knowing neither how to live or how to survive, it will die." Tariq Ramadan, *Islam and the Arab Awakening* (New York: Oxford University Press, 2012), 132–33.

brand of ideology allows for new ways of thinking and acting to emerge on an individual, group, and cultural level without demanding a particular set of dogmatic principles.

Here, ideology does not equate to one kind of philosophy – like communism or capitalism – but instead embraces a variety of beliefs. It allows for different, even competing, perspectives to exist in tandem and even fuse together to create new forms. Ideology, in this sense, is similar to a code of ethics, which guides behavior and thinking and can be applied to a variety of different belief systems.

The Arab Spring embraces this particular kind of ideological discourse, which continues to shape events in the region. It is reflected most clearly in the calls for dignity that dominated the revolutions' earliest days. An ideal concept for many, dignity, or rather the lack thereof, was hardly an abstraction for the people of the Arab world. Mohamed Bouazizi's humiliation at the hands of local police was not a surprising or uncommon occurrence in many Arab countries. Most regional governments had little to no respect for their people, treating them with contempt at worst and indifference at best.

Calls for dignity resulted not from dogmas or particular political philosophies, but rather from a paradigm shift in thinking, namely, a refusal to be degraded and insulted any longer. These demands for respect and dignified treatment mobilized the region's largely depoliticized populations, and emboldened them to refuse to be "sheep in [the government's] herd" any longer.[7]

Dignity was but one of a variety of popular demands, which demonstrate the transformation in mind-set sparked by the Arab Spring. The freedom to speak, think, and act boldly was a strong theme during the revolutions' early days. Armed with a renewed sense of individual self-respect, people collectively declared their unwillingness to succumb to fear or intimidation at the hands of state officials or counter-revolutionary actors.

Transcending differences of creed, gender, age, and socio economic class, unity was also the order of the day at the start of the Arab Spring – calls for social justice, both political and economic, trumped

[7]Noam Cohen, "Egyptians Were Unplugged, and Uncowed," *New York Times*, February 20, 2011, http://www.nytimes.com/2011/02/21/business/media/21link.html.

parochial and partisan divisions. Ethnicity and religion were abandoned, playing no role in the formation or deployment of revolutionary demands. What defined the revolutions, instead, was an ethic of responsibility in which individuals were accountable to one another and to their societies and governments were expected to be responsive to their people.

In the Arab Spring's early day, slogans of dignity, defiance, and unity came from every direction. During Egypt's eighteen-day revolt, banners in Tahrir Square declared, "They shot us with rubber bullets. We will not despair. We will not submit,"[8] "I used to be afraid ...(then) I became Egyptian,"[9] "I would rather die in Tahrir Square than have you govern me and live in humiliation .... You will leave Mubarak,"[10] and "Egypt belongs to all Egyptians, Muslims and Christians."[11] In Yemen's Change Square, similar sentiments were heard, including chants of "No political parties, no partisan politics, our revolution is a youth revolution," and "Our revolution is one of struggle, men and women together."[12] In Libya, the revolution was punctuated with chants of "Libya, Libya, raise your voice! It's our time! It's our choice!" and "Together we will stand! Until he [Ghaddafi] leaves our land!"[13]

Omar Kamel, an Egyptian activist, provides a description of the shift in perspective created in his country during the revolution's early days, which could easily apply to other Arab Spring states: "[W]e had experienced an Egypt that we had never dared imagine; one in which we could all stand together whether rich or poor, educated or illiterate, religious or secular. No matter what our political ideologies might have been, we formed a community of individuals that cared deeply for one another, one in which you knew that the man or woman standing next to you, whose name you did not happen to know, would easily risk his or her life to save yours."[14]

---

[8]Karima Khalil, ed., *Messages from Tahrir: Signs from Egypt's Revolution* (Cairo: The American University in Cairo Press, 2011), 69.
[9]Ibid., 48.
[10]Ibid., 1.
[11]Ibid., 74.
[12]Yemeni revolutionary slogans courtesy of Yemeni activist, Atiaf Alwazir.
[13]Libyan revolutionary slogans courtesy of "Libyan Revolution Chants," http://libyanchants.blogspot.ca.
[14]Omar Kamel, "The Once and Future Egypt," *BRICS Post*, January 25, 2013, http://thebricspost.com/the-once-and-future-egypt/#.UaatSZXuflK.

In reflecting on demands made during the region's various revolutions, other commentators have identified additional aspects of the Arab Spring's new ethos. For Hamid Dabashi, this new ideology includes a "cosmopolitanism worldliness" that emancipated people from and destroyed binaries like West versus East, national versus international, them versus us: "The language we are hearing in these revolts is neither Islamic nor anti-Islamic, neither Eastern nor Western, neither religious nor secular — it is a worldly language, emerging from the depth of people's historical experiences in the world, toward the world, a language irreducible to any familiar cliché."[15]

Islamic scholar, Tariq Ramadan, adds another layer of insight to the Arab Spring's ideological discourse. For Ramadan, the Arab Spring's legacy remains steeped in the region's culture and traditions. He argues that, while messages about freedom, justice, and dignity transcend political and religious discourses, they remain distinctly rooted in the region's history and values. For Ramadan, these traditions are key to ensuring that Arab Spring countries do not succumb to and become dominated by Western ideologies, ways of thinking, and systems of government.[16]

As Ramadan insists, a shift in mind-set does not, and should not, require abandoning one's historical, cultural, and religious reference points. It does, however, provide new insights and perspectives on how these traditions are understood, both in and of themselves and in relation to other traditions. In this sense, while the Arab Spring demands a rethinking of the concept of "ideology," it also requires reassessing different ideological discourses that have long existed in the region, most particularly, Islamism, secularism, and sectarianism.

Historically, these ideologies arose in reaction to Western colonialism or were fueled by indigenous, autocratic regimes usually with help from Western governments. For decades, the region's dictators used Islamism, secularism, and sectarianism to divide and control domestic populations, which often led to political and social discrimination that created long-standing grievances.

While these ideologies had little to do with igniting the region's revolutions, they have hardly disappeared from Arab Spring

[15]Dabashi, *The Arab Spring*, 81–82.
[16]Ramadan, *Islam and the Arab Awakening*, 20–21.

countries. Actors that oppose the region's revolutions or otherwise hold particular political goals have successfully manipulated these ideologies to further their own interests. In a number of cases, these discourses have helped roll back the unity displayed during the revolutions' early days and drown out the Arab Spring's original ethos. Most tragically, these belief systems have frequently distracted from the more important work at hand, namely, shaking off decades of authoritarian rule and creating more inclusive, socially aware, and just societies.

Islamism, secularism, and sectarianism are not, however, inherently divisive or destructive forces. Nor, in many cases, can they be eliminated from Arab Spring countries. Islamism, for example, is very much rooted in religious identities that are important to many people and will inevitably play a role in the region in some form.

To ensure these ideologies serve more productive goals and that the Arab Spring's new ethos takes root, it is important to understand how Islamism, secularism, and sectarianism, in their divisive forms, are currently playing out in the region, and to begin reassessing these concepts. In rethinking these ideologies, the ethos of the Arab Spring, particularly its spirit of civic entrepreneurism, plays an important role. Many of the region's new groups, organizations, movements, and start-ups reflect the values of unity, inclusiveness, and mutual respect embodied by the Arab Spring. They also reflect an additional aspect of this new ethos that is crucial to overcoming exclusionary ideologies, namely, an understanding of collective action and speech as integral to human connection, individual dignity, and political power.

3.2.1 Islamism and Secularism

While often presented as a monolith, Islamism has historically included a diverse set of groups, from political parties to armed organizations. It has also featured a multiplicity of belief systems, from the pragmatism of the Muslim Brotherhood to the dogmatism of some Salafist groups.

Since the start of the Arab Spring, Islamists have made significant gains. In addition to initial successes in Tunisia and Egypt, Islamist groups achieved political prominence in a number of other Arab Spring states. In Yemen, Islah rode the revolution's coattails to success.[17] Long aligned with the Saleh regime, Islah was and remains the country's main opposition party and most powerful and influential Islamist organization. Although it was initially reluctant to support the revolutionary movement, as President Saleh's grip on power began crumbling in June 2011, Islah moved to take a more central role in the revolution. Unlike the youth who had ignited the uprising, the Islamist group was more willing to negotiate with the regime, helping to broker Saleh's resignation and becoming a key political actor in Yemen after his departure.

After years of suffering under the Ghaddafi regime, Libya's Muslim Brotherhood, along with several Salafist groups, has also increased in size and prominence, thanks largely to their critical role during the armed conflict.[18] As a result of this newfound popularity, these groups made substantial gains in the country's parliamentary elections in July 2012.

In some states where Islamist parties have risen to power, the mixing of religion and politics has led to deep social tensions. Perhaps the most troubling of these ruptures has been between Islamist and secularist actors. These divisions have been particularly acute in Tunisia and Egypt where extreme positions have dominated conversations on religion's role in the political sphere. Committed secularists, who refuse to accept Islamist rule, and old school Islamists, who are hesitant to share power with other groups for either ideological or, more commonly, survivalist reasons, have hijacked debates on religion's public role.

These polarizing perspectives have drawn on a decades-long vilification of Islamism by the region's authoritarian regimes. Thanks to this legacy, fears about political Islam have become entrenched to varying degrees in some Arab Spring countries. This has made some people unwilling to tolerate or accept Islamist-led governments. In response, groups, like Egypt's Muslim Brotherhood, have worked to protect their political gains as a matter of survival. This has increased tensions and, in the case of Egypt's Brotherhood, led to substantial political setbacks.

---

[17]Founded in 1990, Islah was born out of an alliance between tribal forces in Yemen's rural areas, the Muslim Brotherhood, which was strong in urban areas, and Salafist sheikhs.

[18]Alongside these groups, small but well-organized extremist elements have begun to emerge. Some of these entities have destroyed various Sufi shrines and even invaded the U.S. liaison office in Benghazi in September 2012.

But, extreme positions taken by some cannot hide the more common and important trends in regional debates on religion's political role. For instance, in Egypt, many Islamists and secularists support the concept of a "civil state."[19] While the term is flexible and accommodates a variety of political visions, in its most basic form the civil state includes democracy, constitutionalism, the equality of citizens before the law, and a public, although undefined, role for religion.[20] In this way, the civil state represents potential common ground between Islamists and secularists that may eventually help repair divisions between the two sides.

Notwithstanding tensions in some countries, in other states, Islamism's divisiveness has been overstated, if not wholly fabricated. This has been particularly true in Yemen where the government has sought to transform its long-standing battle with al-Hirak, a coalition of opposition groups formed in 2006, into a religious conflict.

After armed groups overtook much of the country's southern province while Saleh was still clinging to power in 2011, the beleaguered Yemeni government accused these groups of being Islamic fighters tied to al-Qaeda. In adopting this narrative, the government hoped to win Western support, particularly military aid. Although some groups involved in the secessionist struggle maintained ties with the terrorist organization, the movement was primarily led by al-Hirak, which is unaffiliated with al-Qaeda.

The relationship between the Yemeni government and al-Hirak is complex, and belies attempts to impose religious overtones on the conflict. After its independence from Britain in 1967, Yemen's southern region existed as a separate state until unification with the north in 1990. A civil war ensued shortly thereafter, in May 1994, after political fallout from the unification process resulted in a string of assassinations. After two months of fighting, the conflict ended in July of that year.

Following these events, the central Yemeni government had trouble controlling large swaths of territory in the south as well as parts of the north. To exert control over these areas, the Saleh regime took brutal actions, which created deep-seated resentment among local

---

[19]Peter Hill, "The Civil and the Secular," *Muftah*, February 28, 2013, http://muftah.org/the-civil-and-the-secular-in-contemporary-arab-politics/.
[20]Ibid.

populations. As a result, by the mid-2000s, an insurrection had emerged in the southern provinces, led by al-Hirak. As the 2011 revolution unfolded, Saleh ordered troops stationed in the southern regions and other remote parts of the country to the capital to shore up his power base. Al-Hirak took advantage of this opportunity and extended its control over territory to which it had long laid claim.

As these various examples demonstrate, the role of Islamism and secularism in Arab Spring countries has varied. In some, though not all, cases, these ideologies have either been divisive forces or has been manipulated for political gain. What is true across the board, however, is that religion, especially Islam, is an important part of individual and community identity, as well as daily life. As an extension of the Islamic faith, political Islam has the potential to play a uniting, rather than dividing, role in regional countries.

At the very least, it need not act as a barrier to collaboration. Indeed, in post-Ghaddafi Libya, Islamist organizations have maintained common cause with various non-Islamist groups through bonds forged in war. During the armed conflict with government forces, Islamists worked in coordination with various groups, including tribes and militias, in a struggle defined not by religious ideology but by a desire for freedom and liberty.[21] In post-Ghaddafi Libya, these alliances continue to define relations between various political and social groups, regardless of their Islamist credentials. The same trends can, and should, emerge in other Arab Spring countries as well.

3.2.2 Sectarianism

Over the last few years, sectarianism has increasingly insinuated itself into conversations about the region's revolutions. While some have made absolutist claims about the ideology's supposed rise since the start of the Arab Spring, the real influence of sectarianism has varied between countries. In some cases, sectarian rhetoric and violence have, indeed, experienced a sharp surge since the revolutions began. In other cases, it has been a wholly exaggerated or fictionalized phenomenon. Whether real or imagined, however, sectarianism in Arab Spring countries is less a religious matter and more a reflection of complex political realities.

---

[21]Wolfram Lacher, "Fault Lines of the Revolution: Political Actors, Camps, and Conflicts in the New Libya," Stiftung Wissenschaft und Politik (SWP) Research Paper (German Institute for International and Security Affairs, May 2013).

Events inside Egypt are a prime example of sectarianism's political origins. Amid reigning chaos, violence between confessional groups has found a breeding ground in the country. This has included clashes between Muslims and Coptic Christians, which have occasionally had fatal consequences. Violence has also occurred between Islamic sects. In late June 2013, four Egyptian Shiites were killed in a village in Giza, close to Cairo, after weeks of sectarian incitement by Salafist preachers.

While sectarian incidents are still relatively limited in the country, they are increasing in frequency. What has remained consistent, however, is the state's response. Whether before or since the revolution, government reactions to sectarian violence have eschewed the rule of law. Instead, extra-legal remedies that effectively sweep these problems under the rug have been used. When acts of sectarian violence occur, government officials rarely make arrests or encourage legal redress. Instead, they direct aggrieved parties to pursue reconciliation and other forms of informal dispute resolution, which foster impunity.

These approaches are largely a result of political considerations. For years, the Mubarak regime allegedly abetted attacks against Coptic Christians to strengthen its image as a stabilizing force and defender of minority groups. It also perpetuated state practices that ensured sectarianism would continue, like sustaining the country's neo-millet system and upholding laws that defined Egyptian citizenship in terms of religious membership.[22] Since Mubarak's ouster, these policies have remained unchanged. State security forces have also continued to fan the flames of sectarian violence. In some cases, like the November 2011 massacre of Coptic Christians at Cairo's Maspero television station, state forces have assumed a direct role in fueling armed sectarian conflict.

By failing to address, and in some cases actively supporting, sectarianism, the Egyptian state sows disunity among its people. For a government facing many pressing economic and political challenges this

[22]Long before Mubarak, Egypt had developed a neo-millet system in which parallel institutions and regulations supported the needs of religious minority groups. Rather than benefiting from this system, many religious minorities continued to face state-sanctioned discrimination because of this framework. For instance, Coptic Christians experienced various forms of disparate treatment, including regulations that placed restrictions on building and renovating their houses of worship. Paul S. Rowe, "Neo-millet Systems and Transnational Religious Movements: The Humayun Decrees and Church Construction in Egypt," *Journal of Church and State* 49 no.2 (2007), 239–350.

disunity is a convenient tool, helping to divert public attention from the most important task of all — the battle for freedom and social justice in the country.

In Syria, sectarianism has been a fluid, though disturbing, phenomenon, affected as much by the flow of funds and weapons into the country as by devotion to a particular confessional ideology. Defying easy assessment or glib summary, it is difficult to assess the true force of sectarianism. While it does not appear to define or drive the conflict as of yet, its specter has loomed larger and larger over the country.

This turn of events was not inevitable. Throughout Syrian history, personal identity has reflected a complex web of allegiances that included religion but also extended to family, town, and region. Religious moderation and peaceful coexistence have been far more common than extremism or sectarian conflict. Nor has the Syrian government traditionally relied on religion or ethnicity to shore up support. Instead, it has historically cultivated a political base that spanned sectarian and ethnic divisions, and was far from limited to the ruling regime's Alawite sect.[23]

When the revolution began, however, the government's attitude toward sectarianism changed. From early on in the peaceful protest movement, the Assad regime used sectarianism for its own political ends. In order to divide Syrians and bolster support from minority communities, the regime attempted to misrepresent the revolution as a sectarian uprising.

As the conflict became more violent, some members of the armed opposition also began depicting the struggle as primarily religious in nature. Although they initially represented a slim minority, these groups, which were largely Salafist in orientation, saw the conflict as a struggle against Shiism as represented by the Alawite regime.

In its response to the protests, the government helped perpetuate this narrative. From the earliest days of the revolution, the regime relied on the "most loyal, Alawite-dominated elements of its security forces" to crush the peaceful uprising.[24] When Syria's Shiite allies, Iran

[23]"Syria " *Freedom House*, 2012, http://www.freedomhouse.org/report/freedom-world/2012/syria-0.
[24]"Tentative Jihad: Syria's Fundamentalist Opposition," Middle East Report No. 131, International Crisis Group, October 12, 2012, 8.

and Hezbollah, publicly declared their support for the Assad regime, further credence was given to the Salafist position.

As violence spread, Salafism, which had never been a prominent force in the country, became increasingly attractive to the rural migrant underclass that inhabited many Syrian cities. These individuals, who had suffered economically under the Assad regime, had received little guidance or solace from traditional religious leaders during the conflict. As weeks and months passed by, their hopes for a political or military breakthrough from secular opposition forces were diminishing just as Salafist fighters were making inroads against the regime.[25]

While these sentiments explain some of Salafism's attraction, supporting the sectarian narrative also served pragmatic ends. With wealthy Gulf Arabs eager to fund Salafist fighters in Syria, sectarianism became part of a bidding war. Some armed opposition groups,[26] many of which operated independently, found financial benefit in adopting Salafist styles of dress and appearance and invoking sectarian narratives to obtain much-needed funds from Gulf sponsors.[27]

These developments in Syria are a prime example of how tolerant societies are warped when religion is used as a divisive tool. Acknowledging religious difference does not necessarily lead, however, to divisiveness and conflict. Indeed, these are the markers of a pluralistic society, and the building blocks of any democracy. While "sectarianism" has long been associated with religious discrimination and violence, the concept can, and should, be rehabilitated to embody appreciation and respect for diversity within politically inclusive societies.

Religious differences are not going to disappear from the region, but they must not be used as tools for furthering partisan political goals that fracture national unity.

---

[25]The Salafist fighters struggling against Assad were effective armed groups that appeared to threaten the regime's continued existence. Ibid., 5.

[26]The Free Syrian Army has generally rejected sectarianism.

[27]In Bahrain, the Al Khalifa monarchy used the specter of sectarianism for expressly political purposes. From the start, the regime attempted to dismiss and delegitimize the revolution by casting protesters as disgruntled Shiites working in the service of Iran. The narrative bore no connection with realities on the ground and was even discredited by the BICI's final report.

3.2.3 A Way Forward

To varying degrees, Islamism, secularism, and sectarianism have eroded the Arab Spring's message of unity and inclusion. These concepts are not, however, inherently opposed to the revolutions' new ethos. Not all Islamists are interested in marginalizing members of other religions nor are all secularists opposed to the role of Islamism in the political sphere. Even sectarianism can be a positive force, where it reflects a respect for difference rather than a power struggle between different groups.

The Arab Spring's spirit of civic entrepreneurism can help develop these more inclusive ideological forms. By emphasizing public action and speech, civic entrepreneurship encourages individuals to advocate for more progressive forms of Islamism, secularism, and sectarianism while also embodying the very values of unity and collaboration that can help moderate these ideologies.

Before the revolutions began, most people in the Arab world were hesitant to express their views or mobilize to address particular issues or challenges facing their communities.[28] Some were simply resigned to the status quo, hopeless about the prospects for change. Others were numb to daily injustices, or were simply too busy struggling to make ends meet. In many countries, a small elite reaped the benefits of corrupt government practices and had little reason to push for change.

Where dissent did exist, it was often hidden from public view, confined to the private sphere where speech was little more than "mere talk" and action a means to an end rather than an end itself. Public spaces, where individuals could speak and act in concert with one another, where they could come together to create new realities, in full view of their fellow citizens, were rare and largely non-existent.

The Arab Spring changed all this. From the very start, the force of human action and speech was unleashed in the most public of places – the streets and squares of regional countries. At peaceful demonstrations, gathered together in public spaces, regular individuals, from all

---

[28]There were, of course, exceptions to these trends. Some, though not all, countries impacted by the Arab Spring had active civil society sectors, labor movements, and an increasingly nontraditional and experimental artistic and cultural scene before the revolutions broke out. Still, these phenomena largely existed on the fringes and were fairly limited in terms of their political and social impact.

walks of life, expressed their desires for a better life and, in the process, revealed themselves to one another. As Hannah Arendt explains, "[The] revelatory quality of speech and actions comes to the fore where people are with others and neither for nor against them – that is, in sheer human togetherness. Although nobody knows whom he reveals when he discloses himself in deed or word, he must be willing to risk the disclosure. ... Because of its inherent tendency to disclose the agent together with the act, action needs for its full appearance the shining brightness we once called glory, and which is possible only in the public realm."[29]

In speaking out and taking to the streets, people in the Arab world made their public debut after years of being invisible to the state. It was a process that was both intensely personal and community-oriented, and, at its very core, as mentioned above, about human dignity. As Arendt explains, while dignity may be an individual feeling, it is achieved only through speech and action that take place in relation to other people — whenever this human togetherness is lost, whenever people are "for or against other people," individual dignity dissipates.[30]

Once the Arab Spring began, and the roots of the public realm started to take hold, human connection was created between those who had once been strangers – these bonds were ones founded in speech and action, and not familial or social ties. Indeed, many of those who participated in the revolutions' early days and went on to found various initiatives, organizations, or movements have spoken of how these events created the chance for them to meet, speak, and connect with others for the first time.

This human togetherness also generated political power for all those involved. It is this power "[that] keeps the public realm ... in existence."[31] This concept of power, which rests on a community of individuals speaking and acting together, has been key to the success of the Arab Spring and lives on in the civic entrepreneurism that continues to flourish in the region. As Arendt explains, "What keeps people together after the fleeting moment of action has passed (what we today call 'organization') and what, at the same time, they keep alive through

[29]Hannah Arendt, *The Human Condition* (Chicago: University of Chicago Press, 1998), 180.
[30]Ibid.
[31]Ibid., 200.

remaining together is power."[32] Because power is boundless, the more groups, organizations, initiatives, and other platforms for human connection that exist, the more political power spreads throughout a society.[33]

Because divisive mentalities undermine political power and the public sphere, civic entrepreneurs have little choice but to advocate for policies and ideologies that unite, rather than divide. This means applying the tools of public speech and action in ways that encourage interpretations of Islamism, secularism, and sectarianism that emphasize inclusiveness and unity. Should civic entrepreneurs fail to adopt these behaviors, or promote exclusionary policies and mind-sets, the very circumstances that made their existence possible cease to exist.

Civic entrepreneurship also concretely embodies the power of collaboration and unity. In speaking out in support of more progressive forms of Islamism and other ideologies, civic entrepreneurs can point to their own organizations and groups as reflecting the basic values that undergird this moderation. In this way, the various initiatives that have arisen since the start of the Arab Spring serve as an example to others of what can be achieved through this new mind-set.

3.3 DEMOCRACY

Democracy has long become a hollow term. For many, it symbolizes little more than party politics, supplemented by occasional trips to the voting booth. More often than not, it is also associated with a capitalist, and increasingly neo liberal, set of economic policies, which benefit the few and hurt the many.

The Arab Spring represents a plea for a radical reform of these approaches to democratic government. In its will to action and focus on "Bread, Freedom, and Dignity"[34] the region's revolutions represent a desire for a more participatory form of democracy in which political rights are intimately connected to economic opportunities and social justice.

[32]Ibid., 201.
[33]The interplay between these organizations, initiatives, movements, and start-ups has created checks and balances that generate more power through more human connections without allowing any one group to be more powerful than any other. Ibid.
[34]"Bread, Freedom, and Diginity" was a famous slogan from the region's revolutions.

The elements of this new breed of democracy are not new. Political theorists have long discussed and debated the limitations and pitfalls of representative democracy, in which the masses express their political will primarily through the ballot box. Some theorists, like Hannah Arendt, have explicitly derided this elections-only focus and emphasized the importance of participatory democracy, which demands more direct public engagement in government through public action and speech. The civic entrepreneurism taking place in many Arab Spring countries reflects a desire for this kind of democratic government.

The notion that economic and human rights should be included in any meaningful understanding of democracy is also not an uncommon concept, although it has yet to be fully implemented or embraced by contemporary democracies. Egalitarians have long advocated for governments to provide certain opportunities to their citizens, in areas such as income, education, food, housing, and health care. The "welfare" state, which protects citizens' civil liberties while also providing for their social and economic well-being, is the closest most governments have come to expanding beyond traditional notions of democracy as a set of freedoms and liberties.

What makes the Arab Spring unique is that it combines a desire for participatory government with a call for economic and social justice. This distinctive set of demands emerges from a legacy of political and economic deprivation in countries where autocratic regimes prohibited or restricted collective action and speech, instituted neoliberal policies that reversed state programs that provided economic relief to citizens, and trampled on people's most basic human rights and civil liberties.

But, for some political theorists, like Hannah Arendt, "social" concerns, including economic matters, issues of social justice, and human welfare cannot be part of participatory [or even representative] government since they have no place in public speech and action. Instead, these forces regulate behavior, which encourages conformity, rather than facilitating action, which encourages distinction.[35] According to Arendt, socio-economic concerns and other related activities "serve ... only the purpose of making a living, of sustaining the life process" and are more properly part of the private realm.[36]

---

[35] Arendt, *The Human Condition.*
[36] Ibid., 37.

As the Arab Spring demonstrates, however, economic and social rights are not private matters that thwart human action. Nor are they subordinate to "political" rights. Rather, they are the very product of a vibrant public sphere. Since the Arab Spring began, civic entrepreneurs have demonstrated these facts through campaigns, initiatives, groups, and organizations that address widespread socio-economic problems, such as sexual harassment, domestic violence, poverty, and urban deterioration, among other concerns.

While these problems pre-existed the revolutions, they were "hidden" and pushed into the shadows by authoritarian governments unwilling or unable to tackle these issues. Before the Arab Spring, organized grassroots attempts by civilians to address these problems were considered acts of grave sedition and actively blocked by government officials. Through state suppression and enforced silence, these economic and social concerns became closely connected with related deprivations of political rights. As old regimes fell and public spaces took shape, upending the establishment meant bringing all these issues out from the shadows and into the light of the public arena.

The reasons why economic and social rights took center stage in the Arab Spring are not, however, limited to historical factors. Economic welfare and social justice are concerns of the political man, the stuff of concrete collective action, as well as debate and discussion. Although in their exercise these rights may relate to the "basics of making a living," advocating for socio-economic justice is a collective activity. It requires the give and take of the public realm and is critical to ensuring man's political freedoms are not sacrificed at the altar of social and economic class.

In thinking about the future of the Arab Spring, we must consider whether and how these calls for participatory government, as well as economic and social justice, continue not only on the macro, but also the micro, level. It is in focusing on the grassroots expressions of these demands that attention must be paid to the rise of civic entrepreneurship during the Arab revolutions.

Reflecting the origins of the Arab Spring, these organizations, groups, initiatives, movements, campaigns, and start-ups also act as a shadow government, reminding both the state and society of the values that sparked the Arab Spring, and, in the case of some initiatives, actively pushing back against government policies or actions that undermine or fail to reflect the demands of the revolution.

It is to these groups that we now turn.

CHAPTER 4

Civic Entrepreneurship in Politics and Society

Since the start of the Arab Spring, the most obvious displays of civic entrepreneurship have related to political and social issues. Across the region, people have organized in various forms, often spontaneously, to advocate and lobby for changes to laws, to protest against actions by transitional governments, and to push for social awareness on a variety of issues.

Many of these efforts grew out of demonstrations and public gatherings that dominated the revolutions' earliest days when many burgeoning civic entrepreneurs met for the first time. In some cases, groups that existed before the Arab Spring also discovered opportunities to expand their work in new and unexpected ways after the uprisings began.

Whatever their forms or origins, these initiatives have brought people together from various walks of life for the sole purpose of tackling specific issues. Prior to these experiences, many of these individuals had little to no training in political mobilization. By participating in these projects, they developed these skills while also transforming in other ways. Many discovered an unexpected sense of investment in their country's future, met people they would not have otherwise come across, and found their own distinct voice among the teeming crowds.

This chapter features a small selection of the countless movements, initiatives, groups, and organizations working on political and social issues in various Arab Spring countries. It begins with a look at perhaps the most iconic phenomenon of all: the appropriation and occupation of public squares. It goes on to examine the rise of issue-based movements and citizen-organized local councils. Among the groups and initiatives also discussed here are organizations working to build civil society and youth engagement, initiatives focused on women's issues, public service organizations, and digital platforms that expose various government abuses.

4.1 PUBLIC SQUARES

For thousands of years, public squares have been a literal space for social and political interaction. Sites of debate, discussion, and interpersonal transaction, they have served as a venue for individuals to exchange ideas and goods and otherwise meet and be seen by their fellow citizens.

In modern times, the public square has also become a potent symbol of government authority and a site for displaying state power. Indeed, across various Arab Spring countries, authoritarian governments have tightly controlled these spaces. Libya and Syria were perhaps the most extreme examples, with images of the "leader" and other monuments to the regime dominating these areas. For people in these and other regional countries, this "occupation" of the public square was a daily and mundane reminder of the barriers to engaging in public life and the restrictions on political freedoms.

This was all changed with the Arab Spring. From the very start of these revolutions, the region's public squares transformed from state-dominated products of urban development to physical symbols of popular political engagement. They became the embodiment of people power, giving concrete form to resistance and providing protesters with something durable to defend.

While real, physical places, public squares also became idealized spaces. They allowed people to both imagine and experiment with new forms of human interactions that crossed socio-economic and political barriers. In this sense, they armed those who inhabited or observed these spaces with the inspiration and experience to go out and create new realities in their own communities.

For anyone who has paid even passing attention to the Egyptian revolution, Tahrir Square needs little introduction. Tahrir, which means "Liberation" in Arabic, is a large traffic roundabout situated amid the hustle and bustle of downtown Cairo. After the fall of Ben Ali, Egyptian activists, including members of the April 6 Youth Movement, chose Tahrir as the location for protests calling for an end to police brutality and other government abuses.[1]

---

[1] The 2011 revolution was not the first time Tahrir was the center of protests. The square witnessed its first demonstrations on February 11, 1946, in opposition to the British colonial presence in the country.

When January 25 rolled around, thousands poured into Tahrir from various parts of Cairo, but were forced out by security officials after several hours. Only a few days later, on January 28, massive crowds took complete control over the square and began what would become a weeks-long occupation.

During this period, Tahrir became the physical manifestation of the "public arena," a place where people talked, debated, protested, and slept side by side. From the very first day, microphones and speaker systems were brought in so people could give speeches – cultural and political leaders made appearances in the square to lend their support. It was a space full of humor and joy, where musicians performed songs written for the revolution and where art installations, inspired by the uprising, popped up. Conga lines were formed, and there was even a wedding.

As one observer described Tahrir during this period, "Multiple stages were assembled for concerts, speeches, and poetry readings; tent cities mushroomed. When the Internet returned [it had been cut on orders from the regime] somebody set up a pair of wireless networks called Revolution 1 and Revolution 2. Others assembled a video system and showed movies late at night on an improvised bed sheet screen. The music, drumming, and chanting became an alarm clock, starting up about eight in the morning and persisting throughout the day."[2]

Divisions of gender, creed, profession, and age were immaterial in Tahrir. All that mattered was the cause—ousting Mubarak and reclaiming the people's dignity and national unity. Sexual harassment, a ubiquitous problem in Egypt, was virtually unheard of in Tahrir during this period. Weapons of all kinds were forbidden. Security and cleaning details were created. By the time the president stepped down, a small city had formed in the square – a utopia as some described it – created, maintained, and protected by countless civilians who self-organized and took action.

From the start of the revolution, Tahrir was an enigma for the Mubarak regime. Through its unity, cohesion, creativity, and celebration, "[Tahrir Square's] non-violent, non-militant, joyous, jubilant

[2]Ashraf Khalil, *Liberation Square: Inside the Egyptian Revolution and the Rebirth of a Nation* (New York: St. Martin's Press, 2011), 247.
[3]Dabashi, *The Arab Spring*, 110.

disposition rendered the Egyptian army entirely dysfunctional."[3] Of course, this did not stop security forces and pro-government thugs from attempting to charge the square. It also meant, though, that protecting this sacred space was among the highest priorities for protesters.

Tahrir Square's legacy did not end with Mubarak's ouster. As Hamid Dabashi has noted, "As physical space, urban metaphor, and revolutionary allegory, Tahrir Square is central to the Egyptian − and by extension Arab − uprising. It continues to be a center of revolutionary agitation. Protesters periodically go back to it when demanding, for example, security forces be held accountable for their crimes, or to agitate for parliamentary elections or the specifics of drafting a new constitution, or to demand that the military step aside and allow civilian rule."[4]

Over time, however, a more checkered history began to develop, and the glory of Tahrir faded to some extent. Because of its symbolic importance, the square was targeted by counter-revolutionary forces in ways that undermined the sense of safety it had once embodied. Sexual harassment turned into an increasing problem as systematic attacks against female protesters began to arise in Tahrir. Because protests were held so frequently in the space, security officials also became more adept in their crackdowns. Activists seeking to outsmart police and military forces were forced to hold demonstrations in other parts of Cairo, abandoning the square during some periods.

But, like all things connected with the region's revolutions, things have once again changed − the Tamarrod-led demonstrations that ousted Mohamed Morsi brought Tahrir back onto the scene as the center of revolutionary activity in the country.

As in Egypt, Yemen's protesters also chose to center their revolution around a public square. In the early days of the country's uprising, supporters of President Saleh, who had been watching events unfold in Egypt, rushed to Sana'a's central square, which was also named Tahrir, and occupied the area. In doing so, they hoped to protect the square from opposition control, and to deprive protesters of a potent symbol that had been central to Egypt's revolution. Demonstrators responded by occupying a major intersection outside Sana'a University, and creating their own "public square" which they dubbed "Taghrir Square" or

[4]Ibid.

"The Square of Change." Like its Cairene counterpart, Change Square became "a sociopolitical entity with political festivities, songs, stage plays, poems, exhibitions and dance."[5] At its height, it was filled with tents, housed tens of thousands of activists, and stretched so far that a motorcycle taxi service was set up to run from one end to the other.

By and large, there was a pervasive sense of security within Change Square, a rare feeling for many activists who otherwise risked kidnapping, torture, or secret detention for their actions. Because of its vibrant political and social scene and output of creativity, the square was soon dubbed "the first step toward a civil state" in Yemen.[6] For protesters, the space reflected their collective commitment to continue demonstrating until the revolution's goals had been achieved.

As in Cairo, Change Square was a melting pot, "Tribesmen from the remote mountains and deserts march[ed] alongside urban professionals, and well-off merchants with the unemployed. Shiite rebels from the north and secessionists from the south join[ed] in with dissident soldiers who [had] in the past fought both their movements. Women and men mix[ed] with startling freedom for a country where segregation of the sexes [was] the hard-and-fast rule."[7]

For quite some time, Change Square continued as a physical symbol of Yemen's revolution. As political parties began to infiltrate the space, setting up their own tents and exerting control over the revolution's narrative, things began to change, however. Conservative political groups started segregating women and men in the square, and creating other rules of separation and exclusion that alienated those who had originally established the space. By May 2013, these and other political parties, which had come to dominate the space, decided to abandon Change Square, bringing about its total evacuation amid cries of disapproval from activists.

In Bahrain, yet another public square, the Pearl Roundabout, was at the heart of the country's protest movement. Two days after

[5]"Yemen: A Social Intifada in a Republic of Sheikhs," *Middle East Policy Council*, 2013, http://www.mepc.org/journal/middle-east-policy-archives/yemen-social-intifada-republic-sheikhs?print.

[6]Afrah Nasser, "Change Square Is Empty, But Change Is Still Needed," *The National*, May 6, 2013, http://www.thenational.ae/thenationalconversation/comment/change-square-is-empty-but-change-is-still-needed.

[7]Hamza Hendawi, "Change Square Seeks to Be Genesis for a New Yemen," *Guardian*, November 16, 2011, http://www.guardian.co.uk/world/feedarticle/9949461.

demonstrations began on February 15, 2011, protesters erected a tent city around the square's central monument, a 300-foot sculpture depicting six swords holding a pearl. As described by Toby C. Jones, an expert on the Gulf who happened to be present that day, "The atmosphere was incredible, Bahraini opposition parties were there as were families, food stalls, makeshift medical centers, mobile phone charging stations and a podium for speakers."[8]

Bahraini officials reacted violently to these displays of public action, storming the square on February 17. Demonstrators managed, however, to retake the square, and continued to regulate and organize the area to ensure order and cleanliness. Tents were designated for media and press, to provide food to visitors, and as gathering spaces for artists. People brought their children to the Pearl Roundabout to join in the picnic-like atmosphere. As one Bahraini described the scene, "This is not just a roundabout; this is the place where the seeds of a new and vibrant and all-inclusive Bahrain have been sown. We will emerge stronger from this place. We all want to hold this country just like those pillars that hold the precious pearl."[9]

But, the regime had other plans for the Pearl Roundabout. On March 16, 2011, security forces pushed out protesters once and for all from the square. On March 18, the government tore down the monument. More than two years since its destruction, the site where the structure once stood remains inaccessible, blocked by riot police vans and soldiers, and dotted by signs strictly prohibiting photography.

4.2 LOCAL CITIZEN COUNCILS

During various revolutions over the last several centuries, local citizen councils have been established to facilitate popular participation in politics. The Arab Spring has been no exception to this trend. Across a number of regional countries, committees developed to take the place of governments either unable or unwilling to provide law and order, providing citizens with their first taste of self-rule.

---

[8]Toby C. Jones, "Battling Over the Legacy of Bahrain's Pearl Roundabout," *Foreign Policy*, February 13, 2013, http://mideast.foreignpolicy.com/posts/2012/02/13/battling_over_the_legacy_of_bahrain_s_pearl_roundabout.
[9]Siraj Wahab, "A Peek Inside Bahrain's Pearl Roundabout," *Arab News*, March 5, 2011, http://www.arabnews.com/node/370166.

These citizens did what their governments often struggled to do — organize and govern effectively. This is not to say the local committees brought complete security or organization to people's lives. Indeed, they were far from monolithic or uniform entities and had varied success rates. Nevertheless, these bodies generally served as vehicles for "active" citizenship and gave regular individuals the chance to have their voices heard on issues that concerned their communities.[10]

In Cairo and other Egyptian cities, civilian committees arose during the eighteen-day uprising to provide needed security services and help restore a sense of safety. The sudden absence of police forces from many Egyptian neighborhoods, as well as rumors that the government had intentionally released thousands of imprisoned convicts onto the streets, created a sense of insecurity and chaos for many. In the words of one committee participant, during those eighteen days, "Committees were everywhere in villages and cities. They became the heartbeat of Egyptian society — locally rooted and flexibly organized, informal and voluntary."[11]

While a number of committees disbanded after Mubarak was deposed and the police returned to neighborhood streets, some continued to operate, albeit for different purposes. Generally, the committees that remained active "have a reputation for being advocates for community development and reform as well as neighborhood watches. In the informal settlements dotting Egyptian cities, popular committees have extracted the provision of essential state services — gas lines, lighting and health clinics. Some popular committees go beyond making claims on the state, operating under the banner of 'defense of the revolution.' Assuming a confrontational stance, these committees seek to expose corrupt local officials and identify policemen with records of human rights violations."[12]

In Syria, local citizen councils have emerged mostly in liberated parts of the country where they act as administrative bodies.[13] Filling

---

[10]As at least one study from Egypt has shown, not all committees were internally democratic or inclusive, with some later becoming co-opted by the state. Asya El-Meehy, "Egypt's Popular Committees," *MERIP*, http://www.merip.org/mer/mer265/egypts-popular-committees.

[11]Ibid.

[12]For more on Egypt's popular committees, see El-Meehy, "Egypt's Popular Committees."

[13]For more on Syria's local councils, see Mohammed Ghanem and Ilhan Tanir, "Syria in Transition: An Insider's View," New America Foundation, December 12, 2012, http://www.youtube.com/watch?v=geBUwbwY05o.

the gap left by the regime, the form and function of these councils vary. In general, they provide humanitarian aid, such as food, shelter, and medical care, as well as civic and municipal services, including waste management, education, and police protection. In a few instances, these bodies have become quite sophisticated and include subcommittees to handle issues such as finance and judicial matters. In some councils, members are elected, while in others membership is by appointment only. A diverse range of individuals sit on these committees, including the revolutionary youth who led the initial protest movement, educators, businessmen, and elders. The councils are primarily funded by individuals inside and outside Syria.

While these committees are far from perfectly functioning entities, they are helping to build a new type of governance structure to replace the old Syria, dominated by the Assad regime. Before the revolution, it was unheard of to see the kind of self-government represented by these citizen councils. Because of the country's emergency law, Syrians were prohibited from gathering together in large groups, making organizing of any kind difficult. Since the revolution began, people have freed themselves of these old restrictions and exercised their right to manage their own communities.

As fighting raged between government and opposition forces in Libya, citizen committees were established to run cities and towns liberated from the Ghaddafi regime.[14] As in Syria, these councils organized civic and municipal services, such as security and banking, and relied largely on financial or in-kind donations to support their work.[15] Many of these committees survived the liberation of Libya and have become formal city councils with elected members that managed local administrative affairs.

As in other regional countries, these institutions gave the Libyan people their first experience with direct democracy. They also subverted the state's decades-long effort to use local councils as extensions of the central government. During the Ghaddafi regime, local institutions were either controlled or destroyed by the government through a

---

[14]Wolfram Lacher, "Families, Tribes and Cities in the Libyan Revolution," *Middle East Policy Council*, http://www.mepc.org/journal/middle-east-policy-archives/families-tribes-and-cities-libyan-revolution.

[15]David Zucchino, "Libyan City Grapples with Self-Rule," *Los Angeles Times*, February 27, 2011, http://articles.latimes.com/2011/feb/27/world/la-fg-libya-benghazi-20110228.

pervasive security and intelligence apparatus that reached deep into Libyan society. Ghaddafi's notorious revolutionary committees operated in many neighborhoods throughout the country and were staffed by regime loyalists who spied on regular citizens and ensured that no one threatened the leader's absolute power through words or actions.

4.3 POLITICAL AND SOCIAL MOVEMENTS

Peaceful political and social movements have perhaps been the most visible manifestation of ongoing popular mobilization in many Arab Spring countries. Though they reached unprecedented levels after the revolutions, various political and social movements existed in some regional states before the uprisings began. In some cases, these pre-revolutionary movements laid the groundwork for recent events and created a foundation of civic organizing and solidarity that helped topple regional dictators.

Egypt best epitomizes this phenomenon. During the 2000s, various socio-economic and political movements helped pave the way for the country's revolution. These included a rise in labor strikes across various Egyptian cities, protests among university students and youth groups associated with different political parties, the strengthening of a pro-Palestine solidarity movement, the establishment of the Kefaya Movement[16] and the April 6 Youth Movement,[17] and the emergence of the "We Are All Khaled Said" initiative in 2010.[18] Through these

[16]Though nominally "non-political," Kefaya is an umbrella organization that formed in 2004 and united various political parties, including communists, liberals, and Islamists, around a call for regime change. Although it enjoyed relative success early on, the coalition eventually lost momentum because of state repression and internal dissension, among other reasons. Nadia Oweidat, Cheryl Benard, Dale Stahl, Walid Kildani, Edward O'Connell, and Audra K. Grant, "The Kefaya Movement: A Case Study of a Grassroots Reform Initiative," *RAND*, 2008, http://www.rand.org/content/dam/rand/pubs/monographs/2008/RAND_MG778.pdf.

[17]The April 6 Youth Movement initially formed to support a labor strike at a textile factory in the industrial town of al-Mahalla al-Kubra on April 6, 2008. In the years that followed, the group has continued to engage in both online and offline political activism.

[18]On June 6, 2010, in Alexandria, Egypt, a young man named Khaled Said was beaten to death in broad daylight by plainclothes police. Because of its brutality, news of Said's death circulated quickly, feeding long-standing public anger with police abuses in the country. Wael Ghonim, an Egyptian executive at Google, helped start a Facebook page called "We Are All Khalid Sa'id," which quickly became a central organizing tool for various protests against police brutality over the subsequent months. In the run up to and following January 25, 2011, the page, which had hundreds of thousands of followers, helped spread information about the eighteen-day uprising. Wael Ghonim, *Revolution 2.0: The Power of the People Is Greater Than the People in Power, A Memoir* (New York: Houghton Mifflin Harcourt, 2012), 58–81.

initiatives, Egyptians refined their political organizing skills, received training, and developed activist networks that would be critical in launching the January 25 revolution.

A similar story can be found in other Arab Spring countries. In Tunisia, popular political contestation emerged in the early 2000s. Although the country's opposition parties remained toothless, various associational and professional groups, particularly judges and lawyers, began to push back against the regime's power politics. Internet activism became increasingly common and led to the arrest of a number of bloggers. Demonstrations against the government's neo liberal policies took place more frequently as well. Labor strikes reached a high point in early 2008, and in August 2010, only a few months before the revolution began, young protesters took to the streets of southeastern Tunisia to demand various socio-economic rights.

Yemen and Bahrain were also no strangers to pre-revolutionary civil disobedience, with both countries boasting a long and sustained history of political and social movements of varying strength. Even in Syria, during the "Damascus Spring" of the early 2000s, citizen mobilization developed, albeit in limited form.[19]

Since the Arab Spring began, tracking the popular movements that have come and gone in the region is a daily undertaking. In Egypt alone, there have been countless socio-economic and political campaigns, ranging from calls to remove religious designations from government-issued documents, such as personal identity cards,[20] to a movement advocating for sustainable, organic farming.[21]

---

[19]After the death of Hafez al-Assad in June 2000, Syrian intellectuals and activists began to engage in vigorous political and social debates through various salons and forums in Damascus and other cities. While the movement, which came to be known as the "Damascus Spring" was initially supported by Bashar al-Assad, the regime started to crack down on this political opening by early 2001.

[20]Robert Mackey, "Antisectarian Campaign in Egypt Urges Citizens to Remove Religion from ID Cards," Lede Blog, *New York Times*, April 15, 2013, http://thelede.blogs.nytimes.com/2013/04/15/anti-sectarian-campaign-in-egypt-urges-citizens-to-remove-religion-from-i-d-cards/.

[21]The Bazoor Balady campaign has led various initiatives to support sustainable farming in Egypt, including organizing protests against the use of genetically modified seeds from the multinational company, Monsanto. Kelby Olson, "Monsanto in Egypt: Activists Refuse to Be Human Guinea Pigs," *Muftah*, May 30, 2013, http://muftah.org/monsanto-in-egypt-activists-refuse-to-be-human-experiments/.

Among the most successful Egyptian movements has been the No Military Trials for Civilians campaign.[22] Established in March 2011, the movement opposes trials of civilian protesters before military tribunals, which began in February of that year. Bringing together journalists, activists, lawyers, and other individuals, the movement has demanded an end to these trials, as well as re-hearings in civilian courts for those who have already been convicted. To spread their message, campaign organizers have arranged conferences, contacted relevant individuals and organizations, and created a website where detainees and their relatives can share their stories with the public.

Shortly after being established, the group attracted public attention and eventually grew into a nationwide movement against military trials for civilians. By the time Mohamed Morsi came to office, the campaign had received substantial international press.

Because of this attention, Morsi formed a panel early in his presidency to investigate the issue of military trials for civilians. In line with the panel's conclusions, the president pardoned several hundred convicted civilians in the summer of 2012. In October 2012, Morsi issued a general amnesty, which opened the door to possible pardons for over a 1,000 other individuals convicted or charged before military courts for acts related to the revolution.[23]

Thanks to recent events, the Tamarrod movement has become, perhaps, the most well known of Egypt's various political campaigns. It was created in late April 2013 by a group of young activists to call on Mohamed Morsi to step down as president. The group aimed to collect 15 million signatures in support of its cause and to hold massive protests against Morsi on June 30, the first anniversary of his presidency.

The campaign grew quickly and exponentially, attracting support from a number of political opposition groups, including the April 6 movement. Concerned with Tamarrod's rising influence, the Muslim Brotherhood embarked on a media blitz, criticizing and threatening movement leaders. Security forces also began arresting participating university students under dubious charges, ranging from "spreading

[22]No Military Trials for Civilians, http://en.nomiltrials.com.
[23]For reasons beyond the scope of this book, quite a few civilians have yet to be pardoned.

lies to disturbing the peace."[24] These actions did little to blunt the movement's momentum. By the eve of protests that would ultimately oust Morsi, Tamarrod organizers claimed (albeit without third-party verification) to have received 22 million signatures.[25]

Since the start of Yemen's revolution, the country's youth movement has been at the forefront of events. In addition to calling for the ouster of President Saleh, the movement's demands have grown to include a call for a parliamentary system of government, among other things. By participating in this amorphous group, many Yemeni youth have had the chance to develop as leaders for the first time, with many going on to create various groups and political parties to push back against the establishment and pursue the revolution's goals.

Other novel campaigns have emerged during the Yemeni revolution. These include two "life marches", which took place between 2011 and 2012.[26] The first march, which was an unprecedented event in the country, occurred in December 2011 and came in response to the GCC agreement and its associated immunity deal for Saleh. Demonstrators demanded the immunity deal be overturned and called for prosecution of the president and other politicians. The march, which started from the city of Taiz and ended in Sana'a, also challenged official claims that Yemen's revolutionaries supported the unity government and the GCC agreement and helped revitalize the protest movement in Sana'a. The second life march, which came a year later, was intended to commemorate the first march and followed the same route.

Both marches took several days and were largely made up of pro-revolutionary groups and individuals from the independent youth movement in Taiz. As participants passed through different cities, they

---

[24]Muhammad Hisham Abeih, "Egypt's Opposition Launches New Campaign to Highlight Grievances," *Al Monitor*, May 14, 2013, http://www.al-monitor.com/pulse/politics/2013/05/egypt-opposition-campaign-against-morsi.html.

[25]As of this writing, questions have emerged about the grassroots nature of Tamarrod, with reports suggesting the movement received substantial help from the military as well as wealthy Egyptian business people. Hamza Hendawi, "Disputes Between Morsi, Military Led to Egypt Coup," *Associated Press*, July 17, 2013, http://www.usnews.com/news/world/articles/2013/07/17/disputes-between-morsi-military-led-to-egypt-coup.

[26]Unless otherwise noted, information about the life marches has been provided by Yemeni activist Atiaf Alwazir. Interview with Atiaf Alwazir, May 13, 2013.

were cheered on, greeted by fireworks, and offered shelter and food.[27] Along the way, other protesters joined in, until the marches ended in the capital where many participants were brutally attacked and arrested by security officials.

In Yemen, "institutional protests" also began shortly after the GCC agreement, although the precise starting point is unclear.[28] These protests, which have reportedly continued periodically in the country, have largely been held within the work place, including on military bases, and in small businesses and universities. Carried out by employees and other members of these institutions, demonstrations have often challenged administrative policies and raised financial grievances, among other issues.

Institutional protests have taken place in dozens of institutions in Yemen. While similar to labor strikes, these on-the-job mobilizations are considered to be distinct forms of protest involving little to no coordination, almost no advance planning, and lacking a discernible leadership of any kind. They are, nevertheless, effective. According to one report, in 2011 alone, employee-led protests in Yemen resulted in management changes in eighteen facilities.[29]

Yemen's institutional protests are a direct result of the country's revolution. Emboldened by their experience participating in the protest movement, many Yemenis turned their attention to problems they faced on the job. Their efforts included confronting individual managers or administrators directly connected to Saleh, as well as authority figures who appeared corrupt or took advantage of corrupt practices. As larger-scale demonstrations on Yemen's streets tapered off, the institutional protests brought new life to the revolution, sending a message to the Hadi government that change in Yemen would have to come at the grassroots level, and that Saleh's cronies could not quietly continue running the country.

---

[27]NoonArabia, "Yemen: The Amazing Life March Arrives in Sanaa," *Global Voices*, December 24, 2012, http://globalvoicesonline.org/2011/12/24/yemen-the-amazing-march-of-life-arrives-in-sanaa/).

[28]Unless otherwise noted, information about the institutional protests has been provided by journalist Abubakr Al-Shamahi. Interview with Abubakr Al-Shamahi, May 13, 2013.

[29]Samar Qaed, "Institutional Upheaval in Yemen, Micro Arab Springs," *Yemen Times*, February 18, 2013, http://www.yementimes.com/en/1652/report/2027/Institutional-upheaval-in-Yemen-micro-Arab-Springs.htm.

In Libya, the Libyan Women's Platform for Peace (LWPP) has emerged to unite women, youth, and other groups and help them engage with decision-makers and legal experts on issues relating to the country's democratic transition.[30] Founded in Cairo in early October 2011, the LWPP, which is considered to be a movement rather than an organization, was created by thirty-five Libyan women of diverse backgrounds.

Since its establishment, the LWPP has taken a unique approach to women's rights issues. As co-founder Zahra' Langhi explains, gender is not isolated, but rather intersects with other issues such as class, tribe, and religion. For these reasons, the LWPP does not focus on women's issues per se, but rather advocates for political inclusion and equal citizenship more generally. For the movement's founders, achieving these goals is the best way to guarantee gender equality.

The movement's various projects focus on five areas: constitution making, popular participation in legislative and parliamentary affairs, media, violence against women, and education. Among its most successful projects, the LWPP lobbied the transitional government for a more inclusive electoral law in advance of the country's July 2012 parliamentary elections.

As originally conceived by the interim government, the law created an exclusionary electoral system based on individual and tribal candidate lists. As Langhi explains, this system would have ensured that patriarchal and tribal structures dominated the country's first free and open parliamentary elections. While troubled by the legislation's negative consequences for female candidates, the LWPP approached the issue by focusing on ways to improve the law's inclusiveness.

Together with other NGOs and women and youth groups, the movement staged protests against the proposed legislation. In parallel with these demonstrations, the LWPP identified and commissioned legal experts to draft a new law that was more politically inclusive, and therefore gender sensitive. In its final iteration, the LWPP's draft proposal set aside eighty of parliament's two hundred seats for political parties. It also mandated that these parties use zipper lists that

---

[30]Unless otherwise indicated, information on the Libyan Women's Peace Platform has been provided by co-founder Zahra' Langhi. Interview with Zahra' Langhi, May 29, 2013.

alternated between male and female candidates, giving women a greater chance of winning seats in parliament.

Through its website and organized protests, the LWPP maintained pressure on the transitional government until the new draft law was eventually passed. In the end, over sixteen percent of Libya's parliamentary seats went to women, a number nearly identical to gender distributions in the U.S. Congress.[31]

Described as Bahrain's most "powerful political force," the February 14 movement has been at the forefront of the uprising from the very start.[32] The movement takes its name from the revolution's inaugural day, but its roots lie in the continuing struggle for freedom and democracy in the country.[33] Every decade or so since the 1920s, sudden popular anger at the regime has emerged, followed by public outbursts, then stalemate, and, finally, government promises of reform, which have either failed to materialize or address the root problems of inequality.

Though there was no particular spark this time around, the Arab Spring presented Bahraini activists with an opportunity to rehabilitate their long struggle for political rights. In the beginning, the February 14 movement used the website, bahrainonline.org, to decide by consensus on the protest's central location, ultimately choosing the Pearl Roundabout. After the roundabout was destroyed and state repression went into overdrive, the February 14 movement went underground.

To protect itself, the movement, which was already dispersed, was further decentralized and links were established with Bahraini villages and towns. The February 14 youth coalition was created with affiliate committees established around the country. These committees took responsibility for organizing various forms of peaceful civil disobedience, which were loosely coordinated by the central movement.

Again and again, February 14 organizers have demonstrated their ability to organize public displays of dissent ranging from the mundane

---

[31]"Polls See Women Get Representation in Libyan Parliament," *All Africa*, July 11, 2012, http://allafrica.com/view/group/main/main/id/00017881.html.

[32]Unless otherwise indicated, information on the February 14th movement has been provided by Ala'a Shehabi, a British-born Bahraini and economics lecturer. Interview with Ala'a Shehabi, May 10, 2013.

[33]Toby C. Jones and Ala'a Shehabi, "Bahrain's Revolutionaries," *Foreign Policy*, January 2, 2012, http://mideast.foreignpolicy.com/posts/2012/01/02/bahrains_revolutionaries.

to the deceptively creative. For instance, the movement has organized a "dignity belt" that halted street traffic, has successfully passed fifteen "torches of freedom" from one village to another, and has mobilized family picnics that were held on the front stoops of people's homes, all as acts of peaceful civil disobedience.[34]

While the government dissects the country through various checkpoints, protests continue in towns and villages across Bahrain under the auspices of the February 14 subcommittees. Despite its resilience, the movement still faces serious challenges. Although the group is anonymous and secretive, many organizers have been arrested as a result of heavy government infiltration. It is unclear how much more repression the movement can handle, but somehow the resistance continues, unflinchingly, against all odds.

In Syria, peaceful resistance persists despite an ever-growing armed conflict. In various cities across the country, local coordination committees (LCCs) have been established to organize these efforts.[35] With approximately sixty to eighty committees around the country, LCCs are the largest organized movement of activists on the ground in Syria committed to civil resistance and nonviolent tactics.

As the revolution has evolved, so has the work of these committees. When the LCCs were first established in March 2011, they focused on broadcasting and publicizing information about events on the ground. They published reports about the peaceful protests happening inside the country, as well as the regime's responses. The committees also worked to record and verify death tolls by interviewing family members and obtaining third-party confirmation.

As armed fighting between opposition and government forces has increased, the LCCs have started delivering humanitarian relief. Within individual communities, committees have provided capacity-building services, including helping to rehabilitate schools and facilitating various kinds of skills training. The LCCs actively organize protests and other acts of civil disobedience, creating campaigns to oppose sectarianism and to encourage the adoption of art as a form of civil protest.

---

[34]Ibid.

[35]Unless otherwise indicated, information on Syria's LCCs has been provided by Rafif Jouejati, a spokesperson for the movement. Interview with Rafif Jouejati, June 23, 2013.

Among their various projects, the LCCs have worked to develop a code of conduct for the Free Syrian Army. Created in collaboration with volunteer lawyers, the manual is grounded in international law and addresses issues such as the treatment of civilians, prisoners of war, and cultural heritage sites. Approximately forty-sixty battalions within the FSA have signed onto the code of conduct.

LCC membership is open to any individual committed to the movement's goals, which include opposing sectarianism, supporting the rule of law, and advocating for freedom and democracy. An umbrella organization coordinates with individual committees on an almost-daily basis regarding a broad range of LCC activities; individual committees work with one another as needed.

In an environment where profiteering is not uncommon, the LCCs are staffed by volunteers who are motivated not by personal gain but by a commitment to the revolution's peaceful origins. As described by Rafif Jouejati, a spokesperson for the LCCs, the committees are a critical way of building a society free of dictatorship and tyranny, bound by the rule of law and a commitment to social justice, and grounded in equal respect for all citizens.

4.4 STRENGTHENING CIVIL SOCIETY, SUPPORTING THE YOUTH

In most Arab Spring countries, civil society varied in depth and quality before the revolutions began. In Egypt[36] and Tunisia,[37] formal civil society organizations, including NGOs and other groups, operated

---

[36]Egyptian civil society dates back to the nineteenth century. For much of its history, the country's civil society groups were primarily religious in orientation and complemented the Egyptian government in providing social services to the poor. In 2002, the Mubarak regime enacted a law requiring all nonprofit organizations to register with the Ministry of Social Solidarity or face criminal penalties. The Ministry was given responsibility for approving the activities of civil society groups, was allowed to intervene in their internal affairs, and was empowered to dissolve organizations that received foreign funding or affiliated with international groups without official government permission. Nadine Sika, "Civil Society and Democratization in Egypt: The Road Not Yet Traveled," *Muftah*, May 29, 2012, http://muftah.org/civil-society-and-democratization-in-egypt-the-road-not-yet-traveled/.

[37]During the Ben Ali regime, the state dominated Tunisian civil society, which had been vibrant in the 1970s and early 80s. This included breaking traditional elite patronage networks, which civil society groups had indirectly relied on to influence government policies. Christopher Alexander, "Authoritarianism and Civil Society in Tunisia: Back from the Democratic Brink," *MERIP*, http://www.merip.org/mer/mer205/authoritarianism-civil-society-tunisia.

within an atmosphere tightly circumscribed by *de facto* and *de jure* state control. In other countries, most notably Libya, civil society was nearly, if not completely, nonexistent, stifled by a government unwilling to entertain any form of organized citizen activism or to admit the existence of social problems of any kind.

After the Arab Spring began, some groups took it upon themselves to breathe life into their countries' civil society sectors and, in particular, to support youth engagement in civic and political activities. Under predecessor regimes, young people were often excluded from the public arena – either dismissed because of their inexperience or stigmatized as "disruptive, parasitic forces."[38] The youth, in turn, suffered from general disaffection and indignation toward societies that left them with few opportunities for genuine self-expression or socio-economic mobilization.

With many individuals, especially young people, looking to launch their own NGOs for the first time, there has been a pressing need for training, advice, and other forms of institutional support. Groups like Resonate! Yemen and Shabab Libya have stood up to fill this gap.

Founded in January 2010 by three Yemeni friends, Resonate! Yemen has been a force for nurturing and growing youth engagement in civic and political issues inside the country.[39] Its mission has evolved over time, with the Arab Spring playing an important role in this process.

When it was first created, Resonate! Yemen was focused exclusively on policy issues, specifically on engaging the youth in the government's ten-point reform plan. The Saleh regime had developed the plan in response to international criticism about the presence of active terrorist organizations in Yemen. Because few inside the country were familiar with the government's proposal, Resonate! Yemen decided to spearhead an awareness-raising initiative focused on the youth and aimed at generating ideas for implementing the reform plan at the grassroots level.

---

[38]Samir Khalaf and Roseanne Saad Khalaf, "Introduction: On the Marginalization and Mobilization of Arab Youth," in *Arab Youth: Social Mobilisation in Times of Risk*, eds. Samir Khalaf and Roseanne Saad Khalaf (London: SAQI, 2011), 9.
[39]Unless otherwise noted, information on Resonate! Yemen has been provided by co-founder Rafat Al-Akhali. Interview with Rafat Al-Akhali, May 5, 2013.

With the eruption of protests in January 2011, the ten-point plan came to a halt.

Between February and August of that year, Resonate! Yemen shifted its focus, becoming more overtly political. The organization began working with youth groups in Change Square, helped them formulate their demands and declarations, and provided them with training on participatory democracy.

As co-founder Rafat Al-Akhali recounts, when Resonate! Yemen was first established, the Yemeni youth were largely disenchanted with the political process. Because of the revolution, this state of affairs transformed almost overnight. Suddenly, everyone wanted to play a part in politics and influence government decisions.

In light of these changes, Resonate! Yemen began to develop strategies for sustaining and institutionalizing emerging youth groups. In 2012, the organization launched the "Institutionalizing the Youth Movement" initiative. For its initial cohort, organizers selected ten youth groups from a collection of over 250 organizations, and provided them with the necessary resources, training, and support to develop more permanent institutional structures.

Resonate! Yemen has also worked on a number of other projects. For instance, since 2011, the organization has held various initiatives to bridge the gap between international actors and Yemeni youth, including a series of round table discussions that bring youth activists in Yemen together with international policy-makers to discuss a range of issues. During the February 2012 presidential elections, Resonate! Yemen began conducting election monitoring through a text messaging system. The organization developed this platform itself and has plans to deploy it in future elections.

As it continues to grow and engage in other projects, Resonate! Yemen remains focused on creating an environment where young people have a voice and feel invested in government. In addition to continuing its youth engagement projects, Resonate! Yemen hopes to produce policy briefs and research papers and eventually create a think tank to work on youth-related issues as well as other matters of political and civic importance.

Like Resonate! Yemen, the work of Shabab Libya involves empowering young people and encouraging them to engage in civic and political work.[40] Like its Yemeni counterpart, Shabab Libya has evolved since it first launched during the early days of the uprising in Libya.

Created by two young Libyans living in the diaspora, Shabab Libya was initially conceived as a social media outlet. When the revolution began, obtaining accurate information about events on the ground was challenging, particularly for those outside Libya. With a network of friends and family inside the country, Shabab Libya's co-founders filled this gap, and provided breaking news via Twitter about developments in the country. In a short period of time, the group's Twitter handle had tens of thousands of followers.

After Ghaddafi's fall, Shabab Libya began to pursue projects related to the country's long-neglected youth population. The group, whose name literally translates as "Libyan youth," started to build a presence inside the country. In partnership with other Libyan organizations, Shabab Libya launched the Libyan Youth Forum, which focuses on training young people in political debate. The forum also runs a "youth change makers program" that brings youth together to learn about social entrepreneurship.

Shabab Libya still retains an active media presence, which has been expanded to include the Libyan Youth Voices platform. The project focuses on amplifying the voices of Libyan youth and features personal stories and profiles of young people who have started their own NGOs in Libya.

Moving forward, Shabab Libya will continue to keep one foot inside and outside the country, providing training to youth in Libya while also broadcasting the perspectives and accomplishments of Libyan youth to the international community. As co-founder Ayat Mneina sees things, Libyans cannot let the freedoms they have gained be lost; young people must take responsibility and help move their country forward.

4.5 WOMEN'S ISSUES

Betraying their own biases, various Western commentators have frequently expressed shock at the visible and active presence of women

[40]Unless otherwise noted, information on Shabab Libya has been provided by co-founder Ayat Mneina. Interview with Ayat Mneina, May 13, 2013.

and girls in demonstrations across the region. This sense of surprise has often doubled at the sight of innumerable veiled women who have taken to the streets to demand their rights.

Indeed, women have been at the forefront of the region's revolutions. They have been some of the most active organizers and leaders, both on and offline, from the early days of the Arab Spring. While for some, this political engagement has been a new experience, others have been involved in activism, including on women's rights issues, long before the revolutions began.

Whatever their prior political experience may be, most of the region's women are under no illusions about the problems facing their societies and recognize the work that must be done to protect and support women's roles in the public arena. Patriarchy is, after all, alive and well in the Middle East, as it is in most of the rest of the world. In Arab Spring countries, however, challenges to women's freedoms have historically been rooted just as much in cynical regime politics as in sociocultural biases.

For decades, regional governments manipulated women's rights issues to suit their own self-interests. During the Mubarak era, for example, the demand for women's rights was closely associated with the president's wife, Suzanne. Because of this dynamic, the movement was viewed not as an organic phenomenon that reflected the interests and experiences of regular Egyptian women, but rather as an elitist, political tool that was connected with the state's authoritarian apparatus.

As they had started to do before the revolutions, women in the region are taking back control over their issues and rights. Since the start of the Arab Spring, they have developed their own culturally sensitive and locally focused solutions to deal with gender issues, which draw on the region's rich legacy of indigenous women's right movements.

They have created formal groups and organizations, as well as loose campaigns, to deal with macro-level problems. These initiatives, which respond to local challenges, address a wide range of issues that do not necessarily speak to Western feminism's traditional focus on individuality, reproductive rights, and sexuality. Instead, many of these efforts are connected to wider concerns with political, economic, and social justice, which are often ignored by Western feminist discourses. These initiatives are often visionary ones, imagining a new and better set of opportunities for women in the region.

In leading and joining these groups women have faced, and will continue to face, opposition from social and political forces that prefer they remain outside the public sphere for ideological or partisan reasons. Nowhere is this more true than in Yemen, where a deeply rooted patriarchal culture has long stood hand in hand with the authoritarian state.

During Yemen's revolution, women took to the streets to challenge political deprivations, as well as to call for equal rights between genders. As described by Saleem Haddad, an expert on Yemen, "Women activists throughout the country have insisted on articulating their struggle for equal rights within a broader revolutionary discourse calling for a 'modern, civic state' with 'justice' and 'equality' for all Yemeni citizens, regardless of gender, religion or geography. This statement is simple, but subversive. Through this approach, women activists have placed themselves at the very centre of Yemen's revolution, whose success now hinges upon the role these women will play in the coming years."[41]

By embedding women's rights within larger calls for social justice, Yemen's female activists have connected the revolution's success with support for women's rights. They are continuing to spread this message through political activism and groups, such as the Yemeni Feminist Movement,[42] that raise awareness about gender equality.

In Egypt, various groups have also connected women's issues to revolutionary demands for social justice. This has been particularly true for organizations dealing with rampant sexual harassment, which has been particularly intense in Tahrir Square. After the eighteen-day uprising ended, Tahrir gradually transformed into a symbol of extreme violence and assault against women. Some of the worst reported incidents of sexual harassment have taken place in the square, reaching unprecedented levels between November 2012 and February 2013.

While the precise motivation is unclear, as Tahrir assaults have increased in intensity and frequency, some activists have insisted they

[41]Saleem Haddad, "Women's Rights and Revolution in Yemen: A Local Perspective," *Muftah*, August 2, 2012, http://muftah.org/womens-rights-and-revolution-in-yemen-a-local-perspective/.

[42]Started by Alaa Al-Eryani, a young Yemeni woman, the Yemeni Feminist Movement is an "intellectual movement that focuses on women's rights and aims to improve the status of women in Yemen through promoting gender equality and opposing discrimination." Benjamin Wiacek, "Meet a Yemeni Feminist," May 12, 2013, *La Voix du Yemen*, http://www.lavoixduyemen.com/en/2013/05/12/meet-a-yemeni-feminist/2648/.

represent attempts by the establishment to delegitimize demonstrations through targeting women's safety.[43] Certainly, the sheer scale and focus of these attacks suggest they are more than just incidental extensions of general problems with sexual harassment in the country.

With the Egyptian police failing to prevent these assaults or arrest perpetrators, civilians — both women and men — have pushed back against this harassment and violence and defended women's place in Tahrir. Formed in November 2012, Operation Anti-Sexual Harassment, also known by its Twitter handle, OpAntiSH, provides physical protection to women in order to stop incidents of group sexual harassment occurring during protests in Tahrir.[44] At great personal risk, volunteers wearing reflective jackets collectively intervene in ongoing attacks to rescue targeted women and deliver them to safety.

To facilitate its work, OpAntiSH has various task forces that operate during demonstrations. These include teams that distribute flyers, which raise awareness about the group's work and feature an emergency hotline number where callers can report ongoing attacks in the square. Scouting groups look out for assaults occurring in Tahrir, while other sub-teams are responsible for taking rescued women to safe locations and providing them with first aid, if necessary.

On days where there are protests in the square, the group sets up a control room, usually close to Tahrir, from which it fields hotline calls and provides intervention teams with the locations of ongoing assaults. With a core group of about fifteen organizers, OpAntiSH has between 100 to 200 volunteers on the ground on active days.

OpAntiSH provides a online forum for women who have been attacked in Tahrir to record their testimony and share their experiences of assault with the public. The group rejects the victim blaming that often accompanies sexual harassment and refuses any suggestion that women are responsible for these attacks.[45]

For several reasons, OpAntiSH also makes a point of including women in its intervention team. As group member Yasmin El-Rifae

---

[43]Elisabeth Jaquette, "The Heroes of Tahrir: Operation Anti-Sexual Harassment," *Muftah*, February 4, 2013, http://muftah.org/heroes-of-tahrir/.

[44]Unless otherwise noted, information on OpAntiSH has been provided by group member Yasmin El-Rifae. Interview with Yasmin El-Rifae April 14, 2013.

[45]Elisabeth Jaquette, "The Heroes of Tahrir."

explains, women victims have often been attacked by men claiming to rescue them – by having women volunteers on these teams, OpAntiSH helps allay any fears victims may have about the intentions of their rescuers. Women volunteers also help subvert gender stereotypes about "weak women" needing to be saved by "strong men." Finally, and perhaps most importantly, many women want to join the intervention teams because of their own personal experiences. Quite a few volunteers with OpAntiSH were themselves attacked in Tahrir and rescued by group members – for them, joining these teams is a way both to give back and assert their refusal to leave the square.

OpAntiSH works closely with other groups in Egypt that deal with sexual harassment issues, including Tahrir Bodyguard. Established during the same period (November 2012) as OpAntiSH, Tahrir Bodyguard works to promote a culture that rejects sexual violence of all kinds, including sexual assault.[46]

Like OpAntiSH, Tahrir Bodyguard engages in physical interventions, with gender-mixed volunteer groups, to rescue women trapped in ongoing assaults during protests in Tahrir Square. With eight founding members and an executive committee of fifteen people, Tahrir Bodyguard can have up to 100 volunteers working on the ground on active days.

Among its other projects, the group hosts free self-defense classes in Cairo, featuring martial arts coaches who volunteer their time. The classes aim not only to teach women how to defend themselves, but also to raise awareness about sexual harassment. As the group looks to the future, awareness-raising campaigns are becoming a more prominent part of its work. According to co-founders Dina Hosny and Maria Sanchez Munoz, Tahrir Bodyguard hopes to launch educational programs in schools and universities to tackle issues of sexual assault, as well as women's equality, gender justice, and women's roles in society and public spaces.

4.6 VOLUNTEERISM

In many Arab Spring countries, public service was an uncommon activity before the revolutions broke out. While the reasons for this

---

[46]Unless otherwise noted, information on Tahrir Bodyguard has been provided by two of the group's co-founders, Dina Hosny and Maria Sanchez Munoz. Interview with Dina Hosny and Maria Sanchez Munoz, May 12, 2013.

vary by country, they include: legal barriers, such as laws that prevented group meetings; informal state policies that discouraged private individuals from organizing to address social issues; entrenched class-based social divisions supported and often encouraged by governments; and education systems designed to keep students under constant academic pressure and away from political and social concerns. These circumstances were often exacerbated by civil society arenas plagued by government co-optation and other restrictions. In the few instances when mass volunteerism did take place, it was typically the result of unique political and moral circumstances that were neither durable nor sustainable.[47] Since the revolutions began, however, public service has surged. Once again, local needs have driven this work.

In Egypt, Tahrir Supplies grew out of violent protests in November 2011 on Mohamed Mahmoud Street, close to Tahrir Square.[48] As security officials were shooting protesters with live ammunition and tear gas, calls went out on social media for medical supplies to treat the wounded. Ahmed Abul Hassan, a young Egyptian man who was living outside the country at the time, started a Twitter account to connect those who were requesting medical assistance with those who were offering help. The Twitter handle quickly went viral, reaching 1,000 followers within the first hour. To deal with the surge in requests, Ahmed put out a call for volunteers to join the group. Several individuals, including a number of Egyptians who lived abroad, responded to his request, and Tahrir Supplies began to take shape.

From the start, Tahrir Supplies worked closely with volunteer doctors who were treating injured protesters on the ground in and around Tahrir. In a short period of time, the group developed a database with contact information for these volunteer doctors. During armed clashes, Tahrir Supplies would reach out to these individuals to determine supply needs. The group would then share the list of needed supplies and delivery locations with its Twitter followers and also post the information on its website. Tahrir Supplies would connected those providing

---

[47]For a short time in the early 2000s, the second intifada in Palestine galvanized Egyptian youth, who collected medicine and food on a mass scale to send to the Palestinian Territories. Asef Bayat, "Reclaiming Youthfulness," in *Arab Youth: Social Mobilisation in Times of Risk*, eds. Samir Khalaf and Roseanne Saad Khalaf (London: SAQI, 2011), 60.

[48]Unless otherwise noted, information on Tahrir Supplies has been provided by team member Amira Ayman. Interview with Amira Ayman S., May 9, 2013.

supplies with doctors in the field hospitals that had been established to treat injured protesters.

The group only acted as a pass-through organization and never handled any of the medical provisions itself. Tahrir Supplies also coordinated its work with volunteers at Rescue Team, a group that provided physical protection to those bringing supplies to field hospitals in Tahrir.

After clashes died down in December 2011, Tahrir Supplies scaled back its activities, but has typically reactivated whenever widespread violence has reemerged. The group is but one example of countless informal and formal public service organizations that have been established in Egypt since the start of the Arab Spring. These include efforts like AlHaqanya and Tahrir Doctors. AlHaqanya is a collective of volunteer lawyers and activists that supplies free legal services to victims of human rights abuses,[49] while Tahrir Doctors is made up of physicians who provide pro bono medical services during violent clashes, as well as free trainings that include classes in first aid.[50]

In Tunisia, the group Afreecan is focused on combating poverty and hunger, particularly in marginalized parts of the country.[51] With a core group of approximately seventy volunteers, the organization aims to increase volunteerism among Tunisia's youth. Amine Manai, Afreecan's founder, believes the true impact of the revolution will come through changes in cultural and social assumptions. For its part, Afreecan challenges traditional mentalities by demonstrating the power of public service to positively impact people's lives.

Although it formally registered as an NGO after Ben Ali's fall, Afreecan was founded in 2000 by Manai, who is a medical doctor. During the Ben Ali regime, the group organized medical caravans and other public service trips to parts of the country that were neglected by the government. Suspicious of their activities, security officials and police would often question organization members about these trips.

Since Ben Ali's ouster, the group's work has substantially expanded beyond these short-term, small-scale projects. Now, Afreecan is able to

---

[49]Al-Haqanya website, http://alhaqanya.blogspot.com.
[50]Tahrir Doctors website, http://tahrirdoctors.com/midandoctors/.
[51]Unless otherwise noted, information on Afreecan has been provided by founder Amine Manai. Interview with Amine Manai, May 27, 2013.

launch initiatives that address the structural causes behind socio-economic inequality. Increased interest in public service activities has also translated into more volunteers for Afreecan's projects.

Among its various initiatives, Afreecan creates "micro-projects" to help individuals raise funds for small businesses that allow them to live independently and with dignity. Providing support to schools and children in various Tunisian villages and towns is a particularly important part of Afreecan's work. The group engages in school renovation projects and organizes campaigns to obtain needed equipment, like computers. Afreecan has also spearheaded donation drives to purchase books and clothing for school children, as part of a larger effort to encourage parents to keep their kids in school and out of the workforce.

Connecting Tunisians to one another, especially across socio-economic lines, is part of Afreecan's mission to help change mentalities. In this regard, the organization runs cultural and ecological tours that bring Tunisians from the diaspora, as well as the country's large cities, to villages in remote areas. In the future, Afreecan hopes to expand its work in a number of ways. It is exploring the possibility of creating football academies, as well as a series of cultural centers across Tunisia to provide dance, painting, and poetry classes for children and adults. Income from these schools will be used to finance Afreecan's charitable activities.

In Libya, the organization Volunteer Libya is working to create "prosperity and wealth" for the country through public service.[52] Established by several diaspora Libyans, as well as one non-Libyan, the organization was founded shortly after the start of the revolution to help Libyan doctors and nurses living abroad travel to the country and volunteer their services during the conflict.

Since Ghaddafi's ouster, Volunteer Libya has expanded its activities to include projects that encourage youth inside Libya to engage in public service. Under the Ghaddafi regime, problems like poverty and social inequality were largely unacknowledged and ignored in the country. Volunteer Libya aims to raise awareness about these issues by introducing youth to community members grappling with these

---

[52]Unless otherwise noted, information on Volunteer Libya has been provided by co-founder and CEO Wafia Sayfalnasr. Interview with Wafia Sayfalnasr, May 20, 2013.

challenges, and giving them tools to develop and implement projects that help address these socio-economic problems.

Wafia Sayfalnasr, CEO and co-founder of Volunteer Libya, sees a desire among Libyan youth to engage in public service projects, and believes in their ability to transform the country. The organization places youth in the driver's seat by giving them substantial influence over its projects. With twenty to thirty core volunteers inside the country, Volunteer Libya's most active youth members propose and select various campaigns for the organization to pursue. In coordination with the group's director of operations, the proposed projects are refined and implemented.

Volunteer Libya has a database of 3,500 volunteers and usually attracts eighty volunteers to each of its events. Among the group's various projects, it has collaborated with several organizations to launch the Save the Old City campaign, which aims to rehabilitate Tripoli's crumbling Old City and provide charitable services to its inhabitants. Through its Kids with Cancer events, Volunteer Libya has worked with various organizations to raise money to renovate and enlarge the children's cancer wing at the Tripoli Medical Center. The group also holds an annual fundraiser during Ramadan to raise money for Tripoli's poor and homeless. In conjunction with the Save the Old City campaign, Volunteer Libya has started its first summer camp for kids in the Old City, which launched in 2013 with a focus on education as well as games, art, and sports.

In the long term, Volunteer Libya hopes to embed public service in Libyan culture and attract all members of society to volunteerism. The organization has drafted a proposal to incorporate public service into the country's educational system through government scholarships awarded to students who engage in charitable activities. While most of its work is currently focused on Tripoli, the group is looking to expand into Benghazi and ultimately throughout the entire country.

Given the near absence of civil society during the Ghaddafi era, collaboration and coordination between organizations within Libya's emerging public service space is critical to cultivating volunteerism. Like Volunteer Libya, Cleaning Up Tripoli has worked with various groups in the country to implement its public service projects. Founded in October 2011, Cleaning Up Tripoli was created by a small group of Libyans, inside and outside the country, with a focus on organizing environmental clean-ups in the country's capital.[53] More broadly, the group's founders aimed to inspire individuals of all ages and socio-economic backgrounds to engage in public service within their local communities.

Since the group first launched, it has organized dozens of clean-ups. Over the course of these projects, participation rates have increased, with volunteers taking part in multiple events. To support its activities, Cleaning Up Tripoli has sought in-kind donations from businesses, government, and civil society. These efforts have largely been successful and have helped increase community investment in the organization's work.

Most clean-ups run by the group last between two to three hours. The organization picks locations that are safe and away from roads, focusing on parks, very large roundabouts, and beaches. Clean-up teams are broken up to cover different areas and assigned discrete tasks, including emptying out garbage cans and distributing water to volunteers. The clean-ups, which usually start in the afternoon, finish before dark so people can travel home safely. A doctor is typically on site to administer first aid as needed.

Cleaning Up Tripoli's work is not only about cleaning and beautifying the city, but also about raising environmental awareness. The group tries to arrange media coverage for its clean-ups, and encourages volunteers to speak about their work on television to help inspire environmental stewardship within their communities. Cleaning Up Tripoli also supports other organizations working on environmental issues, helping to promote their events and providing logistical support.[54]

The group has had other equally important, though perhaps unexpected, effects on the local community. According to its co-founder, Khadija Ali, the organization has helped many individuals become more involved in civil society and public service. A number of Cleaning Up Tripoli volunteers have gone on to become prominent members in other organizations or to start their own groups. The

---

[53]Unless otherwise noted, information on Cleaning Up Libya has been provided by co-founder Khadija Ali. Interview with Khadija Ali, May 30, 2013.

[54]Cleaning Up Tripoli organizers worked with individuals from Benghazi to help them launch a sister group, Cleaning Up Benghazi.

organization has also introduced individuals to parts of Tripoli they had never before seen up close and made them more aware of their surroundings.

4.7 INTERNET ACTIVISM

The region's revolutions have first and foremost been the product of offline organizing and mobilization. Durable public spaces, like Tahrir Square and the Pearl Roundabout, created networks that have been more critical to the revolutions' future than any Facebook group or Twitter handle. The Internet has, nonetheless, been important as a venue to disseminate information and mobilize individuals in the region. This has been particularly true when the public arena has been heavily circumscribed, whether before or after the start of the Arab Spring.[55]

By giving citizens new ways of organizing, as well as accessing and disseminating information, the Internet has and will continue to play an important role in mediating the relationship between citizens and the state in the Arab world.[56] The Tunisian site, Nawaat.org, which was established before the Arab Spring, is one of the most influential online platforms involved in this work.[57] Created by several Tunisian activists and dissidents, Nawaat launched in 2004 and has continued to operate since Ben Ali's fall.[58] The site was founded to promote government transparency, freedom of speech, and gender equality, as well as to fight censorship, police brutality, and government corruption.

When Nawaat first began its work, most Tunisian media outlets were closely tied to the regime. With its commitment to amplifying marginalized and dissenting voices, Nawaat quickly became a hub for information on human rights violations and other abuses committed by the government.[59] It provided information and updates on what the

[55]For instance, in the early to mid-2000s, Arab bloggers began forming online networks to circumvent government restrictions on free speech. These bloggers used their virtual platforms to publicize the arrest of activists, police abuse, torture, and other crimes committed by autocratic regional governments. Rebecca MacKinnon, *Consent of the Networked: The Worldwide Struggle for Internet Freedom* (Philadelphia: Basic Books, 2012), 22–23.

[56]Ibid.

[57]Unless otherwise noted, information on Nawaat has been provided by team member Wafa Ben Hassine. Interview with Wafa Ben Hassine, May 17, 2013.

[58]MacKinnon, *Consent of the Networked.*

[59]MacKinnon, *Consent of the Networked*, 21.

government was censoring and how, as well as tutorials about how to evade online censorship and surveillance.[60] It featured stories about individuals being spied on by the regime and interviews with those who had run-ins with security agents or state officials. In supplying this information and coverage, Nawaat relied on citizen journalists who provided many of the articles, videos, and photos that appeared on the site.

Because of its work, Nawaat was soon targeted by the Ben Ali government and blocked inside Tunisia. By the eve of the revolution, Nawaat had become a "one stop consolidator and archive of information"[61] on government repression and activism in the country. Thanks to its army of citizen journalists, during the Tunisian uprising between December 2010 and January 2011, Nawaat was the premier site for information on the protests.

Since Ben Ali's ouster, Nawaat has continued to put pressure on government authorities, and to feature voices critical of the state. Thanks to the revolution, the group is now able to publicly conduct its activities with a staff that regularly heads into the field to do investigative journalism. Nawaat has officially registered as an NGO in Tunisia and has opened its first offices in the country. Since the revolution, the organization has conducted several workshops in various Tunisian cities to train young people in blogging and social media. It has also created a "hackerspace" in its offices where community members can come together, hold meetings, and collaborate on various projects.

In Bahrain, where restrictions on political dissent continue, Bahrain Watch serves as a web-based platform to increase awareness about events happening inside the country.[62] The organization was formed in February 2012 by a group of individuals inside and outside Bahrain to counter the government's claims about instituting various human rights and democratic reforms. The group aimed to expose these misrepresentations by sifting through and synthesizing the wealth of damning information available on the Internet, while presenting the material in an easily digestible form and providing useful context.

[60]Ibid.
[61]Ibid.
[62]Unless otherwise noted, information on Bahrain Watch has been provided by Ala'a Shehabi, one of the organization's co-founders. Interview with Ala'a Shehabi, May 10, 2013.

Since its establishment, Bahrain Watch has applied these strategies to a variety of other projects. These include, but are not limited to: Access Denied, a report that catalogues various actions taken by the Bahraini government to restrict work done by international journalists, NGO workers, and rights activists in Bahrain since the uprising began; and PR Watch, a project that exposes the public relations companies that have worked to influence the media narrative about events inside the country.

Bahrain Watch disseminates its reports via emails and press releases and targets international media outlets in order to reach the widest possible audience. Ala'a Shehabi, one of the founders of Bahrain Watch, believes the organization has been successful both in raising awareness about the regime's practices and in shifting the international media narrative about the revolution. For instance, the PR Watch campaign received substantial media attention, eventually leading some companies included in the report to end their contracts with the government and to formally apologize for having worked with the regime.

Bahrain Watch has a number of other projects in the pipeline and intends to continue working on issues of government transparency until a democratic system is established in Bahrain.

CHAPTER 5

Civic Entrepreneurship in Art and Culture

The Arab Spring has not only been a political, social, and economic revolution; it has also been a cultural and artistic one. From humorous slogans to revolutionary songs and poetry, art and culture have brought people together, amplified voices, and spread the revolutions' messages to a wider audience.

At the same time, the Arab Spring has helped reinterpret how culture and art are produced, who or what controls the process, and the relationship between culture and national identity. In regional countries that have historically had strong, centralized ministries of culture, people are starting to question the state's role in artistic production.[1] In some places, this debate is happening alongside a brewing "culture war" between secularists and Islamists. After years of exclusion from government-run cultural institutions, Islamist groups are asserting their right to engage in and influence the cultural arena. Secular artists and intellectuals, who have long dominated the scene, are fighting back.[2] Protests held by artists, musicians, and others in Egypt in May/June 2013 embodied these dynamics.[3]

Doing art for the sake of art has also found new meaning since the start of the revolutions. In countries where authoritarian regimes circumscribed individual self-expression, restrictions on artistic production were not just limited to political messages – creativity that challenged the cultural status quo or took place outside designated spaces was often discouraged, as well.[4]

Since the revolutions began, artists and other creative types have actively reclaimed cultural spaces and created artistic products that are

---

[1] Sonali Pahwa and Jessica Windegar, "Culture, State, and Revolution," *MERIP*, http://www.merip.org/mer/mer263/culture-state-revolution.
[2] Ibid.
[3] Meir Walters, "Culture as Politics: The Battle Over Representation in Revolutionary Egypt," *Muftah*, June 26, 2013, http://muftah.org/culture-as-politics-the-battle-over-representation-in-revolutionary-egypt/.
[4] Of course, there were exceptions to this rule. Despite censorship and financial restrictions, Egypt's independent art scene was, for instance, fairly vibrant during the Mubarak era. Pahwa and Windegar, "Culture, State, and Revolution."

not subsumed by government agendas. While motivated by different factors, many of these individuals are driven by a desire to bring art and creativity into people's daily lives, to challenge artistic elitism, and to encourage creativity in societies where art, music, and other forms of self-expression have long been denigrated as "hobbies."

Collaboration and collective action have been at the forefront of these efforts. In many instances, artists have finally been able to publicly showcase their talents, and work with like-minded individuals to create artistic and cultural products. This collaboration has not only connected individuals. It has also inspired people to pursue their own artistic and creative interests, which has fueled even more collaborations. In this way, the Arab Spring has facilitated the very process by which art and culture come into being, that is, through interactions among artists, as well as between artists and their audiences.

This chapter profiles a small selection of the many artistic and cultural initiatives and forms of creative civic entrepreneurship that have emerged since the start of the Arab Spring. It begins with a look at the rise of creative resistance, particularly in Syria where this form of activism has been an important, but largely unacknowledged, force. It goes on to profile the explosive rise in graffiti art in various Arab Spring countries. Finally, it examines how theater and film have been used to document and critique the revolutions, and the different ways in which music and dance have featured in the region since the Arab Spring began.

5.1 CREATIVE RESISTANCE

Revolutions have long been propelled by and inspired creative forms of political expression. On a large scale, the cultural and artistic forms that emerged from the Arab Spring have demonstrated the network effect of this creative resistance in two particular ways.

First, as observed by Donatella Della Ratta, an expert on the use of creative resistance in the Syrian revolution, creative activism during the Arab Spring has generated an immediate and visceral response that has helped build support for the cause.[5] As Della Ratta explains, traditional political activism can be difficult and time-consuming, often

5Interview with Donatella Della Ratta, June 17, 2013.

requiring significant investments of time in order to spread messages.[6] Creative resistance, by contrast, reduces and digests complex political concepts into visual and aural products that are straightforward, powerful, and memorable.[7] By using familiar cultural tropes and incorporating irony and satire, creative resistance speaks to the public at large[8] and inspires emotional as well as intellectual responses. This creates a distribution effect that helps messages go viral and reach more people.

Second, creative resistance actually encourages people to participate in the creative-political process. While new technologies help more consumers become producers, creative resistance also inspires people to experiment with creative forms. This is largely due to the medium's accessibility. Regular individuals with little to no artistic training can easily engage in various kinds of creative resistance. This popular participation is, in fact, critical to the success of many types of creative activism. Graffiti, for example, is more powerful in large amounts- the more people adopt the form, the more graffiti there will be. For other kinds of creative resistance, crowd-sourced material is critical; video projects that document various political demonstrations, for instance, depend on footage taken by individuals often on personal cell phones.

These forms of creative activism challenge the ruling establishment, while also revealing the personal side to resistance. Even when creators remain anonymous, their expressive dissent adds nuance to revolutions, revealing how different individuals or subgroups interpret or understand the revolutionary message. The most potent effect of creative resistance comes, however, in its ability to unleash collective joy and humor. The mass expression of happiness and laughter not only raises spirits in the face of persistent government violence. It also acts as a tool for subverting the repression practiced by authoritarian regimes.[9]

For governments gripped by decades of corruption and mismanagement, joyful resistance is both disconcerting and dangerous. Adept at using violence to crush dissent, authoritarian regimes have few other tools for dealing with humor-fueled activism. The repressive nature of

[6]Ibid.
[7]Ibid.
[8]Ibid.
[9]Asef Bayat, "Reclaiming Youthfulness," 56.

these governments is most bluntly exposed when violence is used to silence joy and happiness, leaving these states in an untenable position.

These various aspects of creative resistance have been most apparent in Syria. Creative activism, which was most visible in the early months of the uprising, was arguably the spark that set off the country's revolution.[10] While it has become less frequent since the armed conflict began, creative resistance continues to take place across the country.

Throughout the revolution, instances of creative activism have taken on different forms and have often come at unexpected moments. In one example from May 2011, a group of activists hid several speakers in Damascus' Arnous Square on a busy Saturday afternoon.[11] As people were going about their day, the speakers periodically activated and blared the song, "Go Away Bashar." Around the same time, a group of activists climbed Mount Qasyoun, a mountain that overlooks Damascus, and rolled ping pong balls labeled "Freedom" down into the city's Muhajereen neighborhood.[12] More recently, in Deraa, an anonymous artist known as the "Painter of Horan" has created pen and ink drawings that mock Assad, his ministers, and other government officials, among other images.[13] To share his work, which he carries on a cell phone, the artist braves the regime's checkpoints and snipers to reach safe houses with Internet connections so he can post his images online.

As these and many other examples demonstrate, Syria's creative resistance movement has emerged from the grassroots. As Della Ratta explains, it is also largely led by individuals who are anonymous or use pseudonyms.[14] These creators expend a great deal of time and, in some cases, risk their own lives to produce and share poetry, art, music, and other creative forms with the world. Seeking neither fame nor fortune, these individuals have established an alternative public sphere amid the chaos and increasing violence of the Syrian revolution.[15]

[10]The Syrian revolution began, after all, when political slogans against Assad were sprayed on a town wall.
[11]Interview with Donatella Della Ratta, June 17, 2013.
[12]Ibid.
[13]"The Rebel Painter of Horan: Paintings that Defy Checkpoints, Snipers and Tyranny," *Syria Untold*, May 2013, http://syriauntold.com/en/story/2013/05/24/3179.
[14]Interview with Donatella Della Ratta, June 17, 2013.
[15]Ibid.

Before the uprising began, the regime dominated the public arena, leaving little room for informal, grassroots cultural production. For Syria's creative revolutionaries, resistance in the form of artistic expression has become a way of retaking the public sphere, as well as sharing their views on the revolution and the regime. In this sense, creative resistance is first and foremost about participating in public debates about Syria's present and future.

Many of the country's most prominent artists have, however, been absent from these debates. After the revolution began, Syria's mainstream artistic community fragmented along partisan lines. Whether out of support for Assad or fear for the consequences to their careers, a number of influential cultural figures in Syria refrained from creating work in support of the uprising. Nevertheless, some well-known Syrian actors, musicians, and artists have openly backed the revolution and participated in the country's creative resistance movement. Among the most renowned of these figures is cartoonist Ali Ferzat. With over 15,000 published drawings to date, Ferzat has been creating cartoons in Syria for several decades. While his work has always included a political subtext, beginning shortly before the revolution, the political messages in his cartoons became more direct and overt.[16]

Ferzat's work embodies one of the abiding features of the Syrian revolution – its sarcasm. As he himself observed about the revolution's sarcastic qualities:

> The good thing is that sometimes in the streets where the fighting is taking place, you find people making jokes, their own practical jokes. You would have people walking around with eggplants. Eggplants look dark, like a bomb. So they would pretend it was a bomb and they would throw eggplants at one another, that would be a game on the streets. And you'd have others who take okra – you know, the vegetable – and okra looks almost like a bullet, so they wear necklaces of okra to pretend it's ammunition. And they take the tubes of the heating system and carry them like it's either a Kalashnikov or an RPG. . . . This form of comic, sarcastic resistance, made the regime feel uncomfortable. The beautiful thing is that people are sarcastic towards their pain because they hope.[17]

---

[16]As a result of his activism, masked individuals loyal to the Assad regime attacked Ferzat in August 2011 and broke his fingers one by one. Ferzat was left for dead on the side of the road, but survived the attack. He now lives and works outside Syria. Karen Leigh, "Ali Ferzat's Sarcastic Revolution," *Syria Deeply*, May 19, 2013, http://beta.syriadeeply.org/2013/05/ali-ferzats-sarcastic-revolution/.

[17]Ibid.

Kafr Nabl, a village in northern Syria, has earned international recognition for its sarcastic and satirical slogans about the revolution. During Kafr Nabl's weekly Friday protests, people take to the streets, holding posters with clever, sarcastic slogans directed toward the Syrian regime as well as international figures, like Barack Obama.[18] The town, which was liberated by the opposition in May 2012, even has its own Facebook page where its humorous and ironic messages are shared with the world.[19]

5.2 STREET GRAFFITI

Street graffiti is one of the most effective artistic mediums for staking a claim to public spaces and amplifying individual voices. While it was previously absent from many Arab Spring countries, graffiti has become one of the most popular art forms since the revolutions began. In terms of aesthetics, street graffiti includes many things, from tagging a slogan or name on a wall to producing elaborate and deeply complex murals that take days to create.

At its core, graffiti is where art meets subversion. In the very act of creating images or scripts on public spaces, graffiti artists violate state prohibitions against vandalism. As walls, bridges, and other areas are tagged, governments paint over these images only to have graffiti, whether from the same or other artists, reappear a few days or hours later. In this way, graffiti artists are perpetually engaged in a literal battle over public spaces with the state.

Of course, the images and tags themselves are often subversive in content. During the Arab Spring, graffiti messages have typically reflected political circumstances, including commentary on recent events as well as critiques about on going state actions. In this manner, graffiti represents a way of pushing back against government policies and memorializing and recording history (albeit in a temporary way).

It also functions as a form of dialogue and public debate. While these conversations may often appear to flow in one direction, from artists to viewer, audiences frequently make their responses known

---

[18]Kelly McEvers and Rime Marrouch, "'Conscience of Syrian Revolution' Faces Challenge from Islamists" *NPR*, March 4, 2013, http://www.npr.org/2013/03/04/173442174/conscience-of-syrian-revolution-faces-challenge-from-islamists.

[19]Kafr Nabl Facebook page, https://www.facebook.com/kafar.nobol.

both to the artists and the wider public. Sometimes viewers react by defacing the image or by sharing their own interpretations about the graffiti on blogs or other media. Artists may also engage in conversations or commentary on each other's work by copying and building on one another's creations or by responding with a unique image that references another artist's design. Some graffiti artists explicitly encourage these conversations by providing downloadable versions of their pieces for free online.

Nearly everywhere the Arab Spring has touched down, graffiti art has emerged. In Libya, many of these images commemorate the revolution's martyrs or ridicule Muammar Ghaddafi.[20] In Syria, individuals with little to no artistic background have become spray-can wielding street artists, participating in collective acts of civil disobedience, like Syria's Freedom Graffiti Week;[21] others have become members of "Spray Man," a loose collective of individuals using graffiti as a form of peaceful resistance.[22] In Egypt, street graffiti has experienced perhaps the most profound growth since the start of the Arab Spring. Unlike some other regional countries, the Egyptian graffiti scene predates the revolution, although the movement was mostly underground and quite small then.[23]

The meteoric rise of Egyptian graffiti began on the first day of the uprising. By the time of Mubarak's ouster, eighteen days later, the walls around Tahrir Square had become a veritable gallery of graffiti imagery. Since then, Mohamed Mahmoud Street, near Tahrir, has become a central location for some of Cairo's most iconic graffiti art. Graffiti can also be found in various neighborhoods across the city and is common in other parts of the country, such as Alexandria, where the country's pre-revolutionary graffiti movement largely began.[24]

---

[20]Soraya Morayef, "Tripoli Graffiti: Revolution Street Art in Libya," *Suzeeinthecity*, July 29, 2012, http://suzeeinthecity.wordpress.com/2012/07/29/tripoli-graffiti-revolution-street-art-in-libya/.

[21]During Syria's Freedom Graffiti Week, Syrian artists in the diaspora created stencils that were copied and used by Syrians inside the country. Interview with Donatella Della Ratta, June 17, 2013.

[22]"Graffiti Men of the Syrian Uprising," *Al Arabiya*, July 21, 2011, http://www.youtube.com/watch?v=PvexAQ5g-68; Donatella Della Ratta, "Drawing Freedom on Syria's Walls—a Tribute to 'Spray Man' Nour Hatem Zahra," *Mediaoriente*, April 30, 2012, http://mediaoriente.com/2012/04/30/drawing-freedom-on-syrias-walls-a-tribute-to-spray-man-nour-hatem-zahra/.

[23]Interview with Soraya Morayef, May 21, 2013.

[24]Ibid.

As explained by Soraya Morayef, an expert on graffiti in various regional countries, there are several reasons why graffiti became so popular in Egypt.[25] First, the revolution empowered people and gave them a sense of ownership over public spaces. In this context, the very act of writing one's name on a wall became a political gesture. Second, the international attention on Tahrir Square extended to include the graffiti in and around the area, helping to fuel the movement.

The topics and themes reflected in Egyptian graffiti have shifted according to the situation inside the country.[26] During the SCAF regime, focus was placed on criticizing the military's actions. After Morsi's election, graffiti art began to target the president and the Muslim Brotherhood, as well as prominent figures from the country's Salafist movement.[27] Graffiti has also been used to support certain political and social movements, including campaigns about freedom of expression, sexual harassment, and religious fanaticism.[28] Artists have created murals to honor various figures related to the revolution, from political activists and revolutionary martyrs to victims of police brutality.

While Egypt's graffiti scene has its fair share of individual stars, collaboration has been an important part of the movement's growth and vibrancy. The work of Ganzeer, one of the most well-known Egyptian graffiti artists, demonstrates how individual creators and collaborative efforts often overlap.[29] Ganzeer was one of the earliest practitioners of graffiti art in Egypt and occasionally participated in the fledgling underground movement during the Mubarak regime. With the start of the revolution, he became more deeply involved in creating street graffiti. On the first day of the revolution, Ganzeer spray-painted protest slogans on the back of a billboard dedicated to Mubarak's National Democratic Party. Within a few days, he was producing more intentionally designed pieces, using stencils as well as political messages.

After Mubarak's expulsion, Ganzeer decided to memorialize the martyrs who had died during the eighteen-day uprising. He planned

---

[25]Ibid.
[26]Ibid.
[27]Ibid.
[28]Ibid.
[29]Unless otherwise indicated, information about Ganzeer's graffiti work has been provided by the artist. Interview with Ganzeer, May 15, 2013.

each mural as a large-scale image of the martyr's face and created stencils to facilitate the production process. Ganzeer painted these murals in broad daylight, attracting groups of people who had never before seen anyone make graffiti art. Several bystanders offered their assistance, and the project soon turned into a collective effort with people volunteering to buy paint and create calligraphy for the murals. Many of these volunteers continued working with Ganzeer on other graffiti projects over the following months, and some even became friends. Ganzeer also organized more formal collaborative efforts, including Mad Graffiti Weekend in mid-2011, an event that brought together various artists and creative types to protest the military.

But, not all of the Arab Spring's graffiti art has been about political or social issues – some artists have used the medium to add beauty to landscapes physically pock-marked by months of ongoing violence or to experiment with different aesthetic styles in a public forum. Some graffiti collectives have even worked with local municipalities to create public mural projects to brighten up neighborhoods and bring art into people's daily lives.

Founded in June 2012 in the Yemeni city of Taiz, Colors of Life was created to bring beauty to the city's streets, which had been devastated by months of demonstrations.[30] While the group avoids expressly political themes, it seeks to enlighten and educate people in other ways, including by drawing attention to and honoring Yemen's forgotten artists. Through its large mural projects, the collective also provides training to new artists and gives them a platform to refine their craft.[31]

5.3 VIDEO AND FILM

Throughout the Arab Spring, video has played a number of overlapping and interconnected roles. Most obviously, it has been a powerful medium for disseminating information and sharing news from the ground. As a way of documenting events in real time, video has helped counter government narratives about the revolutions and expose state violence and other forms of repression against protesters. Thanks to

[30]Interview with Sadek Maktary and Manal Alariqi, members of Colors of Light, June 1, 2013.
[31]Ibid.

advances in technology, video has become a weapon for nearly anyone with a cell phone, turning regular individuals into media rebels.

Video has also been used in other ways to creatively subvert the status quo. As a narrative tool, film has long been a vehicle to produce stories and share new ideas. Since the start of the Arab Spring, various groups have harnessed this power and created short video clips and longer films to educate and entertain individuals and inspire public debate. As with other forms of creative resistance, video is able to cut through complicated ideas and get to the essence of a question, issue, or set of events while also engaging the viewer's heart and mind. Various projects that have emerged from the Arab Spring have played on this duality to create experiences that touch the intellect and the soul.

"Top Goon: Diaries of a Little Dictator" epitomizes the intellectual and emotional experience generated by film.[32] "Top Goon" is a YouTube video series launched in November 2011, which uses finger puppets and satire to lampoon and critique the Syrian regime in ways few other projects have been able to accomplish. There have been two seasons of "Top Goon" so far, with the first season running for thirteen and the second for seventeen episodes. The series has generally been very successful, attracting attention both inside Syria and in the Western press.

"Top Goon" is produced by an anonymous Syrian film collective, Masasit Mati. The group formed in August 2011 to present events inside the country in ways that mass media was failing to do Bringing together various activists and artists, from actors to puppeteers to script writers, Masasit Mati is guided by values of peaceful resistance and tolerance and aims to help create an open and inclusive civil state in Syria through the use of satire, humor, and art. These themes are reflected in the "Top Goon" series, which addresses concepts like civil disobedience, a rejection of sectarianism, and social unity.

As with most other organizations that started during the Arab Spring, many of Masasit Mati's members were strangers before coming together to create the collective. Currently, group members are based

[32]Unless otherwise indicated, information on "Top Goon" and its parent organization, Masasit Mati, has been provided by co-founder and series director Jameel Al-Abiad, via translator. Interview with Jameel Al-Abiad, June 14, 2013.

in various countries, with most of the actors and puppeteers still living inside Syria. What continues to unite these dispersed individuals is an abiding commitment to creative resistance that was forged in the crucible of the revolution's early days.

Recently, the group's activism has moved from the computer screen onto the streets – in late January 2013, members of Masasit Mati staged a street performance, called "I Love Acting" that was held during demonstrations in Aleppo, a Syrian city under opposition control. It was the group's first live performance and experience revealing themselves and their true identities to the public.

The project was motivated by the worsening situation inside Syria. As explained by Jameel Al-Abiad, a pseudonym used by the director of "Top Goon" and one of Masasit Mati's founders, live theater has a magical ability to reach out to people in ways media cannot. Group members felt it was important for Masasit Mati to hold a live performance in order to be part of and have a more positive impact on people's experiences on the ground.

In Libya, the Tripoli Human Rights Film Festival was founded toward the end of 2011 to bring the topic of human rights into people's daily lives.[33] With Ghaddafi's ouster, human rights issues could finally be openly discussed inside the country. While some groups started to hold lectures and debates around the subject, festival founders felt film would bring human rights closer to people's hearts and touch them on a more personal level.

The organization's first film festival was held in November 2012. As group member Lamia Ben Halim explains, the event was intended to engage people both on an emotional and intellectual level by pairing films with moderated discussions, which followed each screening. In choosing movies for the festival, group members focused on pieces that were relevant to the situation inside Libya and that aligned with the country's socially conservative culture. In the end, they selected a group of films from around the world, including two short pieces created by Libyans.

The film festival lasted four days and had a substantial turnout, with approximately 250 people attending each screening. According to

[33]Unless otherwise indicated, information on Tripoli Human Rights Film Festival has been provided by co-founder Lamia Ben Halim. Interview with Lamia Ben Halim, May 29, 2013.

Ben Halim, the discussion periods were lively and featured speakers who were well versed on the films' subject matter. Festival organizers were keen to bring children to the event as well and arranged for several school groups to attend movie screenings relating to children's rights.

Moving forward, organizers hope to hold the film festival every two years, to expand to other cities in Libya, and to develop a school curriculum to teach children about human rights. Among their most ambitious goals, festival founders are keen to eventually create a film competition exclusively for human rights documentaries created by Libyan filmmakers.

In Yemen, the independent collective, Support Yemen, has brought filmmakers, web designers, bloggers, and other activists together to document the struggles of the Yemeni people.[34] The group started as a hashtag (#SupportYemen) launched on Twitter in connection with a social media campaign to raise awareness abroad about events that were taking place during the revolution's early days.[35] Since then, Support Yemen has become a more formal organization and has spearheaded various social justice and grassroots advocacy campaigns in the country.

As part of its work, Support Yemen has created beautifully produced and powerful videos to complement its various projects. The group's first video, which was dedicated to its "Break the Silence" campaign, came during the uprising's early days, and emphasized the Yemeni people's resistance and resilience against government violence.[36] For its "Women's Rights" campaign, Support Yemen created a video that focused on demands made by women protesters, including calls to end systematic gender oppression and patriarchy.[37] The group also produced videos for "Invisible Casualties," a campaign that discusses the community-based impact of the drone war in Yemen. In the future, Support Yemen hopes to launch more grassroots advocacy campaigns that connect offline activities with accompanying videos.

---

[34]Unless otherwise indicated, information about Support Yemen has been provided by co-founder Atiaf Alwazir. Interview with Atiaf Alwazir, May 14, 2013.
[35]Ayesha Chugh, "Media & Revolution: An Interview with Rooj al-Wazir of #SupportYemen," *Muftah*, April 16, 2013, http://muftah.org/supportyemen-mediarevolution-interview/.
[36]Ibid.
[37]Ibid.

As co-founder Rooj Alwazir explains, through its short films Support Yemen has been able to challenge "dominant media representations of Yemen through storytelling, which fosters dialogue and debate, and builds confidence and radical hope within [Yemeni] communities."[38] For Atiaf Alwazir, another co-founder, the goal is for Support Yemen's videos to have a real impact on policy-makers inside Yemen, as well as those outside the country who deal with Yemen-related issues. She hopes the group can also inspire others throughout Yemen to create their own advocacy campaigns centered around film and video.

Since the revolution's earliest days, the Egyptian organization, Mosireen, a non-partisan, independent film collective, has been using video to raise awareness, educate, and enlighten Egyptians about political and social issues inside the country.[39]

Like many other groups, Mosireen took shape in response to developments on the ground. At the end of February 2011, after Mubarak's fall, the military forcibly broke up a sit-in in Tahrir Square and arrested numerous activists. Mosireen was formed in reaction to these events, with group members creating video campaigns about individuals (including their friends) who had been detained by the military.

On a broader level, Mosireen's founders saw their perspectives and that of many other activists excluded from mainstream discourses about the revolution. They believed the group could help fill this gap by making short video clips about important events or issues while also providing a physical space where people could come together and learn how to create their own video narratives. Mosireen has also created an archive to house footage from protests, demonstrations, and other revolutionary events, which the public can access and use for non-commercial purposes.

As the uprising has evolved, Mosireen's work has adapted to changing circumstances. During a popular sit-in in Tahrir Square in July 2011, the collective began holding outdoor screenings. The footage shown during these events was primarily raw and unedited, and featured incidents that had occurred that day or film clips taken from the organization's archives. These viewings came to be known as Tahrir Cinema and have since been held periodically.

---

[38]Ibid.
[39]Unless otherwise indicated, information about Mosireen has been provided by co-founder Khalid Abdalla. Interview with Khalid Abdalla, May 31, 2013.

In October 2011, after military officials brutally crushed demonstrations outside the Maspero television in Cairo, Mosireen created a video about the massacre, which featured clips filmed by citizen journalists that exposed the army's culpability in the violence. The group launched a YouTube channel to publicize and share the video. A few weeks later, security officials violently cracked down on protests in Mohamed Mahmoud Street, prompting the organization to produce more videos about these events.

As co-founder Khalid Abdalla recounts, during this period Mosireen became more than a small collective – it transformed into a network of seventy to ninety people filming, editing, and producing dozens of videos at a fast pace. It was during the events of Mohamed Mahmoud Street that Mosireen's YouTube channel took off and eventually became the most watched non profit YouTube page in the world.

Shortly after the violence in Mohamed Mahmoud came to an end, Mosireen held a Tahrir Cinema event that screened edited and produced videos from these events. At the end of the evening, the group gave the films away. The following day, other people began holding their own screenings using Mosireen's videos. This led to the creation of Kazeboon, an independent, nationwide movement of largely outdoor film screenings that sought to expose the military's lies about violence it was perpetrating in the country.[40]

Around this time, Mosireen began holding workshops in various governorates around the country to teach people about the basics of cinema activism, including filming and editing. So far, Mosireen has trained approximately 400 people through this program. The group has also worked with activists in other countries, including Yemen and Syria, and has collaborated with various groups and movements in Egypt.

5.4 MUSIC AND DANCE

From mass sit-ins in public squares to street performances, music and dance have brought joy, humor, and irreverence to the Arab Spring.[41]

---

[40]Kazeboon is a completely separate organization from Mosireen.

[41]Of course, this festive atmosphere was not exclusive to the Arab Spring. During the French Revolution, "People deployed traditional festive occasions and symbols ... or used political uprisings as occasions for festive behavior." Barbara Ehrenreich, *Dancing in the Streets: A History of Collective Joy* (New York: Metropolitan Books, 2006), 188.

In the face of brutality and repression from security forces, the festive atmosphere created by outbursts of dance and music has helped keep people on the streets. These events have raised energy levels and hopes, staved off fear and doubt, and strengthened popular faith in the revolutions. Music and dance have also acted as a magnet drawing people to the demonstrations, protests, and public squares where their fellow citizens have called for political and social change.

As with other kinds of artistic production, these forms of creative expression have been profoundly shaped by their surrounding political and social environments. This give and take between artistic production and political upheaval has shaped how music and dance continue to evolve in Arab Spring countries, as well as the social and cultural value assigned to these genres.

By and large, the dance and musical trends that emerged during the region's revolutions did not arise out of thin air, but, rather, were rooted in underground or local artistic movements that predated these events. The Arab Spring brought these forms out from the shadows of private homes and small art clubs into the public arena, and, in some cases, gave them the cultural and social legitimacy they once lacked.

In Egypt, *mahragan* or "electro chaabi" music has been an important feature of the country's revolution. Rooted in indigenous festival music, the genre was popularized in 2007 when videos of electro chaabi performances began appearing on YouTube. By the start of the Egyptian revolution, electro chaabi had already evolved from its folkloric roots, although it was still far removed from the mainstream Egyptian music scene. The country's uprising helped transform electro chaabi into a potent form of political and social commentary that some have described as "the edgiest and most explosive music" being produced in Egypt today.[42]

As a way of expressing socio political concerns, the objectives of electro chaabi are simple: "to incite emotion and public comment on life in Egypt, and act ... to instill national pride in the listener. The genre has always carried an attitude of irreverence, humor and sarcasm, as the challenging and cheeky lyrics reveal."[43] Electro chaabi artists have

[42]Ted Swedenburg, "Egypt's Music of Protest: From Sayyid Darwish to DJ Haha," *MERIP*, http://www.merip.org/mer/mer265/egypts-music-protest.

[43]Francesca Baker, "Egypt's Electro Chaabi Music," *Muftah*, June 19, 2013, http://muftah.org/electro-chaabi/.

applied this attitude to their songs about the revolution, which have poked fun at revolutionary mores and slogans while also reflecting how people, especially the working class, feel about the ongoing protests.

While electro chaabi musicians may have been the uprising's Greek chorus, for some artists the revolution has also been a springboard to greater popularity and cultural influence inside and outside Egypt. Once consigned to local celebrations and derided by the elite for their lower and middle class roots, electro chaabi musicians now find themselves on the stage of some of Egypt's most prominent artistic and cultural venues.[44]

Among the other musical styles that have featured prominently in the Arab Spring, hip hop has perhaps been the most documented and discussed. As a genre, hip hop originated in the 1980s in New York City where it was used as a tool of political resistance by young people of color to push back against government practices, like police brutality.[45] At the same time, hip hop was also used as a way to express pride in one's self and community.[46] As explained by Lara Dotson-Renta, who writes on the use of hip hop during the Arab Spring, the medium has always been a way of broadcasting personal narratives that are absent from or ignored by mainstream discourses.[47] Refusing to let others tell or own their stories, hip hop artists speak about their lives, communities, and struggles while addressing various social, political, and economic issues.

While the hip hop industry in the United States has undergone radical transformations over the last thirty years, the genre remains preternaturally democratic in its accessibility, portability, and low production costs.[48] In its focus on personal stories and language, it is inherently adaptable to local cultures, mores, and languages.[49]

While many rap artists in the Arab world have been influenced by American hip hop stars, like Jay Z and TuPac, Arab hip hop reflects the genre's malleability and global accessibility. Many Arab rap songs

---

[44]Ted Swedenburg, "Egypt's Music of Protest."

[45]Interview with Lara Dotson-Renta, Assistant Dean/Assistant Professor at Quinnipiac University, June 12, 2013.

[46]Ibid.

[47]Ibid.

[48]Ibid.

[49]Ibid.

reference local cultures and values in ways that have transformed this imported medium into an indigenous creation. This strong tradition of Arab hip hop music predates the region's revolutions by several years. In some countries, such as Morocco, the hip hop scene extends back to the late 1980s. In many other parts of the Arab world, hip hop appeared on the underground scene between the late 1990s and mid-2000s.

Despite hip hop's political roots, before the Arab Spring many artists in authoritarian countries, such as Egypt and Tunisia, did not incorporate direct political messages into their music. Instead, their songs focused on topics like family, love, and personal (non-political) struggle.[50] After the Arab Spring began, however, the region's hip hop scene was overtaken by revolutionary fervor. From Tunisia to Egypt to Syria, hip hop artists began performing songs that responded to events on the ground and addressed pressing political and social issues.

Among the most iconic rap songs to emerge from the Arab Spring's early days is "Rais Lebled." Released in November 2010, one month before the country's revolution, it was written by a then-obscure Tunisian hip hop artist, El General, and featured lyrics denouncing the Ben Ali regime and decrying its negative impact on Tunisian society. While it immediately became an underground sensation in Tunisia, after the protest movement began the song's popularity exploded, with many referring to it as the anthem of the Arab Spring.

Like Rais Lebled, other hip hop songs emerging from regional the region's revolutions have reflected political circumstances and helped fuel popular mobilization. Through this music, local hip hop artists have engaged in public discourses on a range of issues with their fans, the state, and other musicians. In some cases, these songs have traveled beyond national borders and resonated with listeners in other regional countries.

Hip hop artists from different Arab states, as well as the diaspora, have also worked together to create music about the region's revolutions. These collective efforts are as much a result of the Arab Spring's

[50]Libya's Ibn Thabet was among the few Arab hip hop artists who performed overtly political music before the Arab Spring. His songs attacked Ghaddafi's rule while praising the Libyan people and culture. Ulysses, "Hip Hop and the Arab Uprisings," *Open Democracy*, February 24, 2012, http://www.opendemocracy.net/ulysses/hip-hop-and-arab-uprisings.

spirit of collaboration as they are a function of the Arab hip hop scene itself. Before the revolutions began, many of the region's established artists regularly worked with one another, as well as with Arab musicians in the diaspora.

The growth and trajectory of the Egyptian hip hop group, Arabian Knightz, in some ways reflect the story of hip hop in the Arab world before and since the revolutions.[51] Arabian Knightz was formed in 2005 by several young Egyptian rappers who were disheartened by the commercialized and superficial nature of the Arab music scene. As group co-founder Karim Adel recounts, popular music in the region had drifted away from its artistic and socially conscious roots in the 1960s and 70s. Arabian Knightz aimed to revive this tradition and talk about issues that mattered to people's lives.

The group was also driven by a mission to foster global unity and bridge the gap between cultures. To achieve this goal, Arabian Knightz worked to create a movement that spanned the region and connected artists interested in transforming the corrupt Arab music and media industry. Between late 2007 and early 2008, the group launched "The Arab League" with a mission to unite Arab hip hop artists, counter the superficiality of the region's pop music scene, and inform people about social and political issues. Countless individuals joined the League, from prominent rappers like Palestine's Shadia Mansour and Lebanon's Malikah, to filmmakers, writers, reporters, and graffiti artists.

When the Egyptian revolution began a few years later, members of Arabian Knightz were on the scene in Tahrir Square, helping to write chants and performing for gathered crowds. The group wrote various songs dedicated to Egypt's uprising. "Not Your Prisoner," which was written in the early days of the revolution, included footage from the eighteen-day uprising and railed against the Egyptian government, as well as U.S. interventionism in the Middle East over the preceding decade.[52]

---

[51]Unless otherwise noted, information about Arabian Knightz has been provided by co-founder Karim Adel. Interview with Karim Adel, June 19, 2013.

[52]To view "Not Your Prisoner," see http://www.youtube.com/watch?feature=player_embedded &v=schIdC3LdLk.

In Egypt, where the hip hop scene had already existed for several years, the Arab Spring gave established artists, like Arabian Knightz, the opportunity to reach wider audiences, while also inspiring a new generation of rap musicians to strike out for themselves. Still, as Adel explains, the region's revolutions have done little to challenge the corrupt and uninspired mainstream Arab music industry. By and large, Arab hip hop is still an alternative music form, receiving more attention from international than regional media.

Nevertheless, because of the Arab Spring, social and cultural perceptions about hip hop continue to change in the MENA region. In Tunisia, for instance, hip hop artists, who were once viewed as thugs and gangsters, have now become the country's new elite.[53] Even Rachid Ghannouchi, the head of the Ennahda party, has expressed his preference for hip hop over the traditional folk music popular in Tunisia.[54]

Rock and pop artists have also found a voice for themselves during the Arab Spring. Egyptian guitarist Ramy Essam burst onto the scene during the eighteen-day uprising after penning an unadorned song addressed to Hosni Mubarak titled *Irhal* or "Leave." Essam wrote the song in Tahrir Square by combining various chants that had been popularized by protesters.[55] He played the song in Tahrir before an audience of thousands who sang along to the lyrics; video of the performance became a YouTube sensation, earning Essam the title of "The Singer of the Egyptian Revolution."[56] Other Egyptian artists also created music inspired and devoted to the uprising, including Mohamed Mounir, a popular singer who released a revolutionary love ballad to Egypt called *Ezzzay* or "How Come?"[57]

In Libya, members of the rock band, Guys Underground, went from the Benghazi underground music scene to the middle of the Libyan revolution almost overnight.[58] Founded in 2008 by a group of

---

[53]Ulysses, "Hip Hop and the Arab Uprisings."

[54]Ibid.

[55]Ted Swedenburg, "Egypt's Music of Protest."

[56]Steve Inskeep, "Ramy Essam: The Singer of the Egyptian Revolution," *NPR*, March 15, 2011, http://www.npr.org/2011/03/15/134538629/ramy-esam-the-singer-of-the-egyptian-revolution.

[57]Elizabeth Blair, "The Songs of the Egyptians Protests," *NPR*, February 11, 2011, http://www.npr.org/2011/02/11/133691055/Music-Inspires-Egyptian-Protests.

[58]Unless otherwise noted, information about Guys Underground has been provided by Hussain Kablan, who joined the band after the Libyan revolution began. Interview with Hussain Kablan, June 17, 2013.

young students, Guys Underground mostly performed in universities in Benghazi before the revolution began. As band member Hussain Kablan explains, during the Ghaddafi regime there were few public performance venues. Most musicians either worked on their own or played their music at home among friends and family. Guys Underground was one of the few examples of formal collaboration between musicians in Benghazi during the Ghaddafi era.

While before the revolution the band's songs were not typically tinged with political overtones, one piece, titled "Like My Father Always Says" (auspiciously released a month before the Libyan revolution), subtly touched upon politics by addressing the challenges facing youth in the country. After the revolution began and Benghazi was liberated, Guys Underground produced more overtly political music to support the opposition movement. The group published these and other songs about the revolution on YouTube where it quickly attracted thousands of views.

The band held its first public concert for a large audience in April 2011 in Benghazi. Guys Underground went on to perform in over seventy live concerts in Benghazi and Tripoli that year, gaining exposure that was unimaginable during the Ghaddafi regime. For the group, connecting with a large audience inside and outside the country has always been important. To this end, the band performs in English as well as Arabic and mixes a variety of different genres into its music, including hip hop, heavy metal, and instrumentals. As Kablan explains, Guys Underground wants to be part of the crowd and to connect with its audience on a personal level.

This person-to-person connection between artist and audience is a recurring theme found in many musical and dance efforts since the start of the Arab Spring. From alternative music festivals to street performances, various music groups are bringing their craft directly to the people.

In Egypt, the Oufuqy music festival in Alexandria works to combine different musical genres, to introduce music into people's daily lives, and to challenge false divisions between the mainstream and underground music scenes in the country.[59] The festival features live performances from independent musicians as well as multimedia

[59]Rowan El Shimi, "Alexandria's Oufuqy Music Fest Inspires Alternative to Social Norms," *Ahram Online*, June 25, 2013, http://english.ahram.org.eg/News/74872.aspx.

events, including film screenings.[60] Whether intentional or not, Oufuqy appears designed to facilitate interactions between audience members and musicians and includes a number of artist-led musical workshops. Now in its second year, the festival is organized by Ayman Asfour, who conceived of the event as a place to inspire and nurture independent musicians and connect their work to other genres such as dance, theater, film, and poetry.

Post-Mubarak Egypt has also witnessed a rise in organized, outdoor musical collectives. In Cairo, El Mazzikateya is one of many projects reclaiming the country's streets as a venue for musical production. While government permits are usually required for outdoor performances, like many other groups El Mazzikateya pushes forward with its work, with or without government approval. Although it is clearly challenging the boundaries of Egypt's public spaces, the group is more concerned with raising the status of musicians and bringing enjoyment and fun to people on the street.[61]

Underscoring the motivation behind their work, members of El Mazzikateya explain:

Unfortunately, in Egypt there isn't this [musicians playing in the streets]. We have many artists. We have many musicians. People draw, sing, and play, but they are embarrassed of their profession, and of how people will see them. They are embarrassed about what the street will think. Because of this, we decided that we would go down to the streets.[62]

Alexandria's Mini Mobile Concert reflects similar motivations. Founded in November 2011 by musician Ramez Ashraf, Mini Mobile Concert is a traveling music collaborative that holds small musical events on the streets of Alexandria.[63] As Ashraf describes it, Egypt's artistic scene has historically been self-enclosed and disconnected from the general public. Mini Mobile Concert works to break down this barrier and encourage more artists and musicians to engage in street performances.

[60]Ibid.

[61]Thalia Beaty, "Cairo's Street Musicians: Where Is Your Permit?" *Muftah*, June 15, 2013, http://muftah.org/where-is-your-permit/.

[62]Ibid.

[63]Unless otherwise indicated, information on Mini Mobile concert has been provided by founder Ramez Ashraf. Interview with Ramez Ashraf, May 17, 2013.

The idea for the group grew out of the eighteen-day uprising, which brought many musicians onto the streets to perform for the first time. As Ashraf explains, collaboration between musicians reached a high point during this period, but began to dissipate after Mubarak's expulsion. Mini Mobile Concert sought to push back against this trend, to preserve the creative spirit of the revolution's early days, and to encourage tolerance, unity, and acceptance through music.

Approximately twenty independent musicians are affiliated with Mini Mobile Concert. The group provides each of its artists with equipment for performances, as well as a stable of volunteers to help with organizing and advertising the concerts. In selecting locations, group organizers target unexpected, but busy, pedestrian areas that allow people to gather around the performers. Mini Mobile Concert's first event was held in April 2012 away from Alexandria's downtown area in a relatively poor part of the city.

In organizing its concerts, the group is guided by a respect for local traditions. For instance, performances are organized around the five daily Islamic prayer times to ensure the music stops before the athan, the call to prayer, is announced. As a collective, Mini Mobile Concert does not have a set musical repertoire, but group organizers encourage artists to include classic and even nostalgic Arabic songs in their concerts to draw in passersby.

To avoid being shut down by authorities, concerts are held away from locations with busy street traffic. Rather than steal electricity to run its equipment, Mini Mobile Concert uses its own electrical generators at every event. At the start, transporting these generators and other equipment was the biggest barrier to the group's growth. To resolve this problem, organizers created a tricycle, nicknamed Go'los or "Small Creature," that has a series of drawers containing all the necessary materials for the group's performances.

Ashraf describes the street concerts as creating a positive environment. People slow down when they hear the music and take a few minutes to relax and enjoy the event. The gatherings are peaceful and safe and have yet to be marred by harassment or abuse. In the future, Mini Mobile Concert hopes to hold more performances and to further connect people to the arts.

Founded in March 2012, Danseurs Citoyens ("Citizen Dancers") extends the drive for accessible artistic production in Tunisia by bringing dance to the country's streets.[64] The project was created by a diverse group of professional dancers who were frustrated both with the country's artistic elitism, as well as conservative push back against the arts after Ben Ali's ouster. Their answer to these problems was to take their craft directly to the people.

Many of Danseurs Citoyens' performances are unscripted. To seamlessly incorporate themselves into the daily lives of average Tunisians, group members typically dance in mundane locations in their street clothes. In the past, the group's performances have included a ballerina turning pirouettes between vegetable stands and a break dancer displaying his moves at a bus station among waiting passengers.[65] These and other events are filmed to gauge people's often surprised reactions to these unexpected artistic displays and posted on Facebook and YouTube, where they have been viewed and shared thousands of times. The group's more sophisticated performances occasionally incorporate music and often inspire passersby to join in the dancing. The group also performs at strikes and demonstrations to express solidarity with protesters.

Danseurs Citoyens is part of Art Solution, an organization founded in Tunisia in June 2011. Art Solution supports emerging and alternative art forms that are neglected by Tunisia's official cultural establishment. The organization works primarily in marginalized parts of the country, holding workshops to teach teenagers about dance, graffiti, rap, and spoken-word poetry. Since the group's establishment, approximately 500 children have participated in these workshops.

As Art Solution's co-founder, Bahri Ben Yahmed, explains, the group seeks to emphasize the beauty and hope in life. This message appears to have resonated with many Tunisians who have responded positively to Art Solution's efforts. Still, its projects, including

---

[64]Unless otherwise indicated, information on Danseurs Citoyens has been provided by Bahri Ben Yahmed, one of the project's co-founders. Ben Yahmed also provided information on Art Solution, Danseurs Citoyen's parent organization, which he also co-founded. Interview with Bahri Ben Yamed, May 18, 2013.

[65]Katharina Pfannkuch, "Dancing as Resistance," *YourMiddleEast*, March 4, 2013, http://www .yourmiddleeast.com/columns/article/dancing-as-resistance-video_13178.

Danseurs Citoyens, are not without controversy and have been harshly criticized by some religious conservatives.

Art Solution is currently working to create dance centers in two regions in Tunisia that will provide rehearsal space and hold workshops on the various elements of theatrical production. The group is also producing Tunisia's first movie-length film on dance.

CHAPTER 6

Civic Entrepreneurship in Technology Startups

The concept of entrepreneurship is most commonly connected with the business world, where entrepreneurs are defined as people who create their own income and work for themselves. While the small business person epitomizes the prototypical entrepreneur, individuals like Facebook's Mark Zuckerberg and Apple's Steve Jobs have made entrepreneurship into this century's most celebrated career choice. Thanks to these icons, the business entrepreneur has increasingly been seen as a visionary maverick who disrupts industries through innovative technologies or novel ideas and takes great personal risks to realize improbable dreams.

In the years leading up to the Arab Spring, this brand of rock star entrepreneurship, particularly in the form of technology startups, was peddled around as a solution to the Arab world's substantial economic challenges. This approach was supported by various international institutions, including intergovernmental organizations, like the World Bank, and foreign governments, most notably the United States. Public-private partnerships, like the U.S.-North Africa Partnership for Economic Opportunity (PNB-NAPEO), a joint creation of the U.S. State Department and the Aspen Institute, targeted university-educated youth and created programs and workshops to teach individuals in the region about the benefits of entrepreneurism.

But, in many regional countries becoming an entrepreneur was both an unfamiliar and highly risky proposition for young people who had hoped to secure stable jobs in government or multinational corporations. These risks were compounded by a lack of infrastructure to support the kind of high growth, scalable technology startups advocated by international actors. In some states, Internet connections were still weak and unreliable. Manufacturing sectors that could provide needed materials or produce a company's hardware were often few or nonexistent. Still, international players, as well as some regional governments and institutions, continued to present entrepreneurship as a solution to the Middle East's economic woes.[1]

Ironically, it was a different kind of entrepreneurism that would forever transform the region and spark the Arab Spring. Like many others in the Middle East and North Africa, Tunisia's Mohamed Bouazizi was a self-employed entrepreneur in the informal economy doing work for which he was vastly over-qualified. According to one study, there are over 180 million undocumented entrepreneurs, like Bouazizi, in the Arab world.[2] Alongside small business people and technology rock stars, these individuals, who have been forced into self-employment because of faltering or failing national economies, have long existed but largely been ignored by advocates of entrepreneurism in the MENA region.

After the Arab Spring began, the missionaries of entrepreneurship redoubled their efforts, with some presenting entrepreneurism as a way of preventing further Bouazizis. Despite the irony and thanks, in part, to the euphoria and hope of the revolutions' early days, young people in the Middle East began to flock to the world of entrepreneurship and technology startups. Many started to pursue their own ventures, participate in the region's increasingly common startup competitions, and join business incubators and accelerators, which were starting to crop up in various regional countries.

Since the Arab Spring began, numerous business analysts, technology investors, and development practitioners inside and outside the region have noted the growing wave of technology startups in the Arab world. While many university students and recent graduates have looked to these entities as a solution to scarce job opportunities, for some the appeal goes beyond having one's own business, generating impressive profits, or one day becoming the Mark Zuckerberg of the Middle East.

In a number of these cases, the turn to tech startups has been part and parcel of the public action, collaboration, and collective work that

[1]For some countries, like the United States, entrepreneurship was also seen as a way of bringing incremental political reforms to regional countries and reducing the number of disenfranchised youth with limited economic options who were considered a recruitment base for terrorist organizations.

[2]Alia Mahmoud, "What Do Entrepreneurs in Tunisia Need Most? Legal Reform," *Wamda*, February 15, 2012, http://www.wamda.com/2012/02/what-entrepreneurs-in-tunisia-need-most-legal -reform.

has defined the Arab Spring. While they may be a questionable panacea for the Arab world's economic malaise, the region's tech startups are an important part of the Arab Spring's spirit of civic entrepreneurship. Startups are inherently about linkages and networks, whether between the members themselves or between the startup and its audience. Of course, not all the region's tech startups aim to bring about political change or make a social impact. Those that do, however, represent yet another avenue for participating in ongoing political events and contributing to the improvement of local communities in the MENA region.

As these entities demonstrate, civic entrepreneurship in the Arab world is taking place in ways that go beyond traditional forms, such as NGOs or political movements. Understanding this, creates a deeper appreciation for how the Arab Spring has played out in regional countries and how its ethos of collaboration and collective action manifests at the grassroots levels. The region's tech startups may not be setting up tents in public squares or painting their messages on street walls, but they are providing their members with a space to join together to act and express their voices in the public arena.

This chapter profiles six startups that reflect the Arab Spring's spirit of collaboration. While they all revolve around technology, they also represent a range of different industries and include for-profit businesses, social enterprises, and nonprofits. Most importantly, they reflect the symbiotic relationship that exists between the Arab Spring and segments of the region's emerging startup scene.

6.1 SAPHON ENERGY

Hassine Labaied and Anis Aouini were already exploring the idea of starting a sustainable energy company when demonstrations in Tunisia unexpectedly broke out.[3] At the time, Hassine, a banker, was living in Dubai, while Anis, an engineer, was in Tunisia.

The two men had been friends for nearly twenty years, and, in 2009, had started a consultancy company focused on advising the oil and gas industry on health and safety issues in Tunisia. Anis was, however, becoming increasingly fascinated by the sustainable energy sector.

[3]Unless otherwise noted, information about Saphon Energy has been provided by CEO and co-founder Hassine Labaied. Interview with Hassine Labaied, June 21, 2013.

Soon, the two friends decided to switch gears. They moved away from consulting, and focused, instead, on researching and developing innovative technology solutions for the world's energy problems. Within a few months, in 2010, they registered two international patents, one for a device that would become the "Saphonian," a new kind of wind turbine.

When a large, nationwide march against Ben Ali was announced for January 14, 2011, Hassine decided to fly to Tunisia and participate. He arrived in the country around 3 pm on the day of the march, shortly before Ben Ali's abdication. Anis picked his friend up from the airport. After failing to reach the main demonstration on Habib Bourguiba Street in Tunis, the two men went up to the mountains to catch a glimpse of the march. For both Anis and Hassine, witnessing these events was an emotional experience.

The next day, the country was officially closed for business as people poured onto the streets to celebrate Ben Ali's departure. But, Anis and Hassine had different plans. The two men spent the day in a garage working on the prototype for the Saphonian. A few months later, Hassine officially quit his job in Dubai and moved to Tunis to focus on building their new company, Saphon Energy. The two men would eventually be joined by several other team members, some of whom, like Hassine, left behind lives in other countries to move back to Tunisia and work on building this green technology company.

The Saphonian, a zero-blade turbine that converts wind energy into electrical energy, is the company's centerpiece. By applying innovative technologies, the Saphonian addresses problems that have long-plagued the sustainable energy sector. The prototypical wind turbine features blades that rotate to capture wind, which it converts into electricity. Most experts agree, however, that this method of wind conversion is inefficient (a lot of energy is lost because of the blades), expensive (because of the material used to build the turbines), and has negative ecological impacts (the devices are noisy, hazardous to birds, and cannot be used in densely populated areas).

In developing the Saphonian, Anis, its creator, aimed not to improve bladed turbines, but to replace them with something completely different. In creating his new design, Anis drew inspiration from one of the most basic human innovations − the sail. Wind sails have long been considered the best method for converting wind energy into mechanical energy. The challenge for Anis was to create a sail-inspired design that produced electrical, rather than mechanical, energy.

He solved this problem by giving his sails a unique type of motion known in mechanics as 3D-knot motion. Using this brand of movement, Saphonian "sails" perform a figure eight, involving both horizontal and vertical movements. As a result of this innovation, the device is not only less expensive and more ecologically friendly; it is also 2.3 times more efficient than a traditional three-bladed wind turbine

Armed with this new technology, Hassine and Anis have ambitions to turn Saphon Energy into a global powerhouse in the sustainable energy sector. Ultimately, the two men hope to position their company across the value chain as a utility provider in Tunisia, as well as a manufacturer and licensor of the Saphonian technology to companies in other parts of the world. This drive to become the largest company in Tunisia has not just been fueled by the bottom line. It is also grounded in the founders' passion for reviving their country's rich heritage and contributing to its future.

The company's name speaks to the first of these drivers — saphon is derived from "Baal Saphon," the name given in Carthage to the god of wind. Tunisia is the land of Carthage, a civilization that dominated the western Mediterranean for eight centuries before being brutally snuffed out of existence, as well as the history books, by the Roman Empire.

Carthage was a scientifically advanced society, and a leader in technological experimentation. Saphon Energy aims to remind Tunisians of their Carthaginian roots, which have long been absent from the country's national narrative. For the company's founders, this ancient civilization not only symbolizes innovation and entrepreneurship, but also represents a counterbalance to the history of colonialism that has scarred Tunisian society.

For the Saphon Energy team, Ben Ali's ouster also created a sense of individual responsibility and investment in the country's future. The company's success is very much tied to the contributions it makes to the local community by providing jobs, as well as inspiration, to young people. As Hassine explains, starting a venture and being an entrepreneur in Tunisia come with many challenges. The infrastructure to support businesses, especially technology companies, is lacking, with few private or public institutions supporting research and development or providing seed funding for startups. Perhaps even more daunting, however, are the cultural and psychological barriers to becoming an entrepreneur. Overcoming social expectations that define success as working for a government or large company can be difficult. Without high-profile examples of successful Tunisian entrepreneurs it can be hard for young people to see themselves at the helm of their own businesses.

Hassine and Anis hope their story can help motivate more Tunisians to take on the highs and lows of entrepreneurship, to believe in themselves, and to know they are as capable as anyone else of turning nebulous ideas into concrete realities. As far as Saphon Energy is concerned, the founders insist it will continue to challenge conventional wisdom about renewable energy and develop radical inventions to address climate change issues and provide clean, affordable energy to Tunisia, the region, and the world in the years to come.

6.2 18 DAYS IN EGYPT

Egypt's eighteen-day uprising in January/February 2011 has entered the history books as an iconic symbol of grassroots activism and citizen journalism.[4] The startup, 18 Days in Egypt, aims to tell the story of the Egyptian revolution, from those eighteen days to the present, and to ensure the people who lived and participated in these events have ownership over its narrative.

18 Days in Egypt was founded by Yasmin Elayat, an Egyptian-American new media artist and technologist, and Jigar Mehta, a former data journalist for the *New York Times*, based in the United States. As the revolution was unfolding, Yasmin and Jigar wondered what would happen to all the footage and images people were taking of the protests and other related events. As they were bouncing around ideas, they hit on the notion of using these materials to create a ninety-minute feature film documentary about the uprising.

To gather video and photos for their project, Yasmin and Jigar launched a website shortly after Mubarak's downfall, in late February

[4]Unless otherwise noted, information on 18 Days in Egypt has been provided by co-founder Yasmin Elayat. Interview with Yasmin Elayat, June 20, 2013.

2011, and requested that people add an "#18DaysInEgypt" tag to any relevant footage on YouTube and other sites. As they began using the tag to aggregate content for their film, Yasmin and Jigar realized they would be unable to confirm and verify all the photos and videos without contacting the creators. The two friends also began to wonder whether the documentary format would facilitate the kind of community-based storytelling they wanted to create. Yasmin and Jigar decided they needed to provide people with a platform to directly share and produce their own stories. Soon, they switched gears and began creating a trans-media storytelling website about the Egyptian revolution that was collaborative and citizen-fueled.

By this time, Yasmin had moved back to Egypt from the United States and was working to put together a team to make the project a reality. 18 Days in Egypt partnered with a local tech company to build its storytelling platform and began looking for funding to sustain its work. 2011 turned out to be a good year to be a transmedia startup. The Tribeca Film Institute launched its new media fund that year, and the Sundance Film Institute created a one-week lab for transmedia projects. Yasmin participated in both initiatives, which provided 18 Days in Egypt with seed funding and other support. On January 25, 2012, the revolution's one-year anniversary, 18 Days in Egypt launched its new citizen story-telling platform.

In its current iteration, the site guides users through a step-by-step process to create stories about particular events related to the Egyptian revolution. Once initial data is gathered, including information about the date, time, and people involved in the event, the site gives the story-maker tools to collect further information from Facebook, Twitter, YouTube, and other social media portals. To tell a multimedia story, this content is combined together, and includes links to the original source materials as well as any text added by the user. More than half the stories on the site are in English, others are in Arabic, and some are posted in both languages. Approximately forty percent of users are located outside of Egypt.

As with any kind of community-based project, outreach and community management are critical. For these reasons, 18 Days in Egypt created a fellowship program made up of students, activists, citizen journalists, and others to connect with different communities in the country. Fellows have worked to reach a wide swath of Egyptians and to capture stories from people who are on the margins or cannot access the site thanks to low Internet penetration rates in the country. Fellows have documented these stories through recorded interviews, which are then uploaded onto the site.

In the documentary world, 18 Days in Egypt has done something completely new, giving citizens the tools not only to create their own stories, but also to contribute to a larger narrative about their country. Having gathered over 1,000 stories so far, 18 Days in Egypt is considering next steps for development. The team is exploring ways of converting stories on the site into multi-linear narratives, which allow people to weave through, dig deeper, and engage in a more cinematic way with the site. The group is also looking to create data visualizations to make sense of the larger narrative behind all the individual stories the site has captured.

As Yasmin explains, since the country's revolution began there has been a noticeable rise in new groups and organizations, including start-ups like 18 Days in Egypt. While the ecosystem to support self-directed activity and projects had been missing, since the revolution Yasmin has seen a rise in accelerators and incubators to support and nurture Egyptian startups. Different entrepreneurs are also coming together to form networks to help one another with their initiatives. As Yasmin puts it, collaboration and mutual cooperation have become the order of the day in Egypt's startup community.

6.3 WADEENY

Wadeeny is a perfect example of the cross-collaboration and cooperation that is happening between startups and other organizations in Egypt.[5] Launched in August 2011, Wadeeny was created by two young computer engineers, Aly El Guezery and Hesham Ghandour, to provide carpooling services in Cairo. As Aly explains, traffic can be deadly in Egypt, with countless individuals dying in car accidents every year. Traffic jams also contribute to increased inefficiency, as people spend hours during the workweek in transit. For Hesham and Aly, carpooling is a step toward alleviating some of these traffic problems in Egypt's busy capital.

[5]Unless otherwise noted, information on Wadeeny has been provided by co-founder Aly El Guezery. Interview with Aly El Guezery, June 19, 2013.

While Wadeeny does not provide transportation services itself, its web and app-based platforms allow users to connect with one another to create carpool rides. Once users log on, they can search for the trips they need. If a relevant and active option appears, the user can send a request to the trip creator to join the carpool. If the appropriate option cannot be located, the user can create her own trip and wait for others to join. When a carpool is selected the user pays the car owner through the Wadeeny platform, using credits that are obtained either through online credit card payments or door-to-door cash on delivery courier services. Wadeeny takes a commission on these payment transfers.

Wadeeny's users are largely young people, between the ages of eighteen and thirty-five. Even within this cohort, however, many are hesitant to carpool. The concept is still fairly unusual in Egypt, and, with gas prices still quite low, most people do not feel a pressing need to adopt the practice. Safety and trust concerns also create barriers to user adoption. Wadeeny attempts to address this last challenge by integrating its platform with Facebook so that users can see the friends they have in common. The company also gives women the option of creating female-only trips, which has been one of its most popular features so far.

Although the idea for Wadeeny pre-dates the revolution, the company's co-founders were motivated by the country's political changes to implement their idea and help their local community. It is this drive to solve problems that affect people's daily lives that keep Aly and Hesham committed to their work. Wadeeny contributes to its local community in other ways as well. During demonstrations in Cairo, for example, the company partnered with Tahrir Supplies to help facilitate the delivery of needed goods and materials to field hospitals.

In the short term, Wadeeny is working to integrate its platform with universities and companies to provide carpooling to their members. In the long-term, the company hopes to expand its services beyond Cairo to other large cities in Egypt and eventually to other parts of the globe.

6.4 SOURIALI

SouriaLi is a non profit, grassroots, independent, Internet-based radio station dedicated to fostering an advanced level of awareness about the meaning of civil society, active citizenship, women's empowerment, and youth activism among Syrians.[6]

The station is part of the RO'YA Association, which was founded in August 2012 by four Syrians, Caroline Ayoub, Iyad Kallas, Mazen Gharibe, and Honey Al Sayed. Honey was a recognized radio personality inside Syria, but was forced to leave the country for political reasons in early 2012.

SouriaLi aims to help heal Syrian society and lay the building blocks for a new country. SouriaLi, which means both "Syria is mine" and "surreal," serves as a platform for all Syria's people, no matter what their ideology or political opinion, to engage in open discussion on a variety of topics.

Amid media propaganda and increasing violence inside Syria, SouriaLi works to counteract extremism of all kinds and provide the Syrian grassroots with a forum to begin reflecting on issues critical to reconstituting the country's social fabric. To facilitate this work, SouriaLi's programming focuses on issues like reconciliation, healing, and political inclusion. The station, which launched its beta version in October 2012, talks about the various ethnic and religious groups living in the country, and profiles parts of Syria that have traditionally been marginalized.

SouriaLi's philosophy of inclusion and pluralism also applies to its internal structure. Team members come from different backgrounds, have diverse political leanings, and hail from all parts of the country. Women make up fifty percent of the SouriaLi team because members believe women should have fifty percent representation in Syrian politics.

Although station headquarters are in Cairo, the SouriaLi team, which includes journalists, marketing experts, radio professionals, and others, works from various countries, including a small underground studio in Damascus. In addition to its Internet presence, SouriaLi broadcasts some of its programming on FM radio inside Syria through a partnership with Alwan radio station in the town of Idlib.[7]

---

[6]Unless otherwise indicated, information about SouriaLi has been provided by co-founder Honey Al Sayed. Interview with Honey Al Sayed, June 19, 2013.
[7]For more on the Alwan radio program, please see the station's Facebook page, https://www.facebook.com/AlwanFM.Sy?fref=ts.

Within months of launching, the Syrian regime blocked SouriaLi's web page.[8] Nevertheless, in a short time period, the station's listening audience has grown to 12,000 returning unique listeners from inside and outside Syria.

SouriaLi's programming currently revolves around nine shows. *SouriaLi News Brief* is a satirical news program, similar to *The Daily Show with Jon Stewart* in the United States, and critiques all sides of the revolution. *Hakawati SouriaLi* features stories about civil resistance in Syria and profiles people who have experienced notable successes in the country.[9]

Fattoush is a cooking show that aims to remind Syrians of their roots and rich cultural heritage by using food to tell the history of different parts of Syria. In light of the situation inside the country, the show's producers try to choose recipes that are easy to make, inexpensive, and seasonal.

Days of Pearl discusses culture, tradition, politics, and stories from different eras in Syria's past. The program reminds listeners of the good moments in the country's history, profiles earlier events that hold lessons for Syria's future, and covers the many diverse regions in the country.

Better Syria is a short motivational segment communicating values like unity, inclusion, hope, and faith. *Dialogue* is a program that features discussions with experts on issues like democracy, reconciliation, and freedom of speech. *Misconception* uses humor and sarcasm to discuss the many misunderstandings and biases that are rife in Syrian society now and in the past. *Fanaat* profiles stories of creative resistance in the country and discusses innovative art and culture in Syria's past and present.[10]

As members of the SouriaLi team focus on growing the station, they remain driven by the overarching goal of reaching Syrians inside the country to spread messages of hope, moderation, and inclusion.

---

[8]SouriaLi is also blocked in Jordan and Turkey.

[9]*Hakawati* is inspired by a traditional figure in Syrian culture: the man who sits in the coffee shop and recounts various tales and allegories to bring the community together.

[10]In addition to these programs, SouriaLi also features exclusive interviews with important individuals on topics relevant to the country.

6.5 SYRIA UNTOLD

Launched in May 2013, the website Syria Untold shares stories about creative resistance taking place during the Syrian revolution.[11] The site was founded by Enrico De Angelis and Donatella Della Ratta, two Syria experts involved in documenting efforts at creative resistance in the country. Together with a group of Syrians, based both inside and outside Syria, they have created a platform that focuses on the artistic, creative, and non violent aspects of the opposition movement neglected by the mainstream Western media. The Syria Untold team believes in the importance of telling and sharing these stories in order to present a holistic narrative on the conflict and remind outside observers of the revolution's non violent roots.

Syria Untold amplifies stories of creative resistance already being shared on social media sites and provides the necessary context to understand these events, both as discrete occurrences and parts of a larger, unfolding revolution. Currently, Syria Untold's day-to-day activities are run by a group of individuals that include writers, technologists, and content curators. Since team members are based all over the world, work is coordinated over the Internet and ranges from brainstorming about product development to pitching storylines to feature on the site. Because of the ongoing conflict, group members inside Syria often face challenges with Internet access, as well as the general risks associated with working on a project of this nature while living in the country.

As team member Leila Nachawati recounts, it can be difficult to speak about civil disobedience when people inside Syria are living under the constant threat of physical violence. But the perseverance of Syrians, and the various examples of peaceful resistance taking place inside the country, helps the Syria Untold team remain committed to its work. To those who criticize the group's focus on artistic and creative activism, Leila argues it is through these initiatives that the new Syria will be built.

In addition to reaching those outside the country, Syria Untold hopes to create bridges between Syrians on the ground and grassroots organizations engaging in peaceful resistance in the country. To cater

---

[11]Unless otherwise indicated, information on Syria Untold has been provided by Leila Nachawati. Interview with Leila Nachawati, June 4, 2013.

to its international and domestic audiences, Syria Untold currently publishes its content in both Arabic and English. Though still in its early days, the group hopes to expand its team, aggregate more content from around the Internet, and publish stories in additional languages.

For Leila, a Syrian who lives outside the country, Syria Untold has been a liberating and enlightening experience, allowing her to openly speak about the human rights situation inside the country for the first time. Leila describes the revolution as re-orienting her priorities. Now, she celebrates the small victories, like the occasional peaceful demonstrations in Damascus, and values having her voice, as well as the long-silenced voices of so many Syrians, heard at long last.

6.6 QABILA MEDIA PRODUCTIONS

Qabila Media Productions is an Egyptian startup that creates animated video content to bridge the gap between education and entertainment, with a particular focus on topics such as political science, history, economics, and culture.[12] To date, the group's work has included creating a citizen's guide to politics among other civically oriented video productions.

Qabila was founded before the revolution as an informal group of volunteers that focused mostly on producing video segments on Arab civilization and heritage. In creating Qabila, these individuals were motivated by their frustrations with the Arab media industry. As cofounder Perihan Abou-Zeid explains, Arab media in Egypt and elsewhere was historically biased and shallow, providing very little educational information to listeners. Qabila was established to fill this void.

After the revolution began, Qabila's trajectory shifted. Mubarak's overthrow gave the group an opportunity to broaden its focus to topics, like politics, that had previously been off the table. The revolution also presented the Qabila team with the chance to become a formal business. Before the revolution, media content providers in Egypt

---

[12]Unless otherwise indicated, information about Qabila Media Productions has been provided by CEO and co-founder Perihan Abou-Zeid. Muftah Editors, "Crowdsourcing Content: An Interview with Perihan Abou-Zeid of 'Qabila Media Productions,'" November 12, 2012, *Muftah*, http://muftah.org/crowdsourcing-content-an-interview-with-perihan-abou-zeid-of-qabila-media-productions/.

were required to obtain the approval of state security services in order to operate. This legal requirement was dropped after Mubarak's ouster, which allowed Qabila to incorporate.

Qabila's first video was the initial installment of its citizen's guide to politics. The video was posted on the company's YouTube page where viewers were encouraged to provide feedback and suggestions for future pieces. Qabila has continued to elicit community comment on its content through social media sites, such as Facebook, and often taps into ideas from viewers to create its videos.[13] Once a concept is chosen, team members get to work researching the proposed topic, writing scripts, and doing animation and voice-overs. On average, clip production takes about one to two weeks.

Qabila's team includes animators, directors, marketing experts, and others with a diverse array of political views and backgrounds. Qabila's viewership, which comes primarily through social media, is substantial. Media organizations and other entities inside and outside Egypt use the company's content for educational and other purposes. In the future, Qabila hopes to expand its work to other Arabic-speaking countries. In fact, it has already developed a substantial viewership in Saudi Arabia and produced content about Libya. The company also has ambitions to expand beyond animated and short videos to create documentaries and feature films.

---

[13]Ethar Shalaby, "Qabila TV: A Simple Way to Know All About Politics," *Hiwar Magazine*, December 26, 2011, http://hiwar.dedi.org.eg/highlight/qabila-tv-a-simple-way-to-know-all-about-politics/.

CHAPTER 7

Conclusion: Will Spring Be Eternal?

Since the start of the Arab Spring, the surge in civic entrepreneurship in the MENA region has been unique in size, scope, and frequency. This does not mean, however, that the future is secure for regional states and their popular uprisings. Those interviewed for this book have spoken of the many challenges their countries continue to face and the problems and conflicts that threaten to engulf their respective revolutions.

At the same time, because of their involvement in various kinds of civic entrepreneurship, many interviewees expressed hope and optimism both for their local communities and their countries at large. They spoke about the pre-revolutionary days as a time when they would often toil alone, whether doing art or making music or dreaming about a better future for their country. Then the Arab Spring happened, and, for many, these feelings of isolation began to dissipate.

Through civic entrepreneurship, these individuals have seen the tangible results of their collective action and witnessed the positive effects on their communities as well as themselves. The experience of pursuing a shared goal with like-minded people has given many a deep sense of connection to their fellow group members and volunteers. Through these initiatives, friendships have been formed and lifelong bonds made.

While some of the initiatives profiled here have or will transform into formal organizations, institutions, or startups, most will exist only for as long as they are necessary. This is the nature of public action. Although individual projects and activities may come and go, other initiatives to address the same or other problems will inevitably emerge to take their place. It is through this dynamism that the public sphere will remain healthy and vibrant in Arab Spring countries, and that the rot and stagnation so often plaguing modern societies will be prevented.

As the revolutions head into their fourth year, the rise and fall of these movements, groups, organizations, and startups will continue to be profoundly important to the inclusiveness of the public sphere. In the face of growing violence, sectarianism, and other exclusionary forces, these entities embody the sense of civic responsibility, collaboration, and renewal that is key to ensuring the revolutions' goals of bread, freedom, and dignity are realized.

These groups represent a microcosm of the kinds of society in which their members hope to live, providing a space where they can experiment with new ideas, try different forms of collective action, and, above all, remain connected and united to one another.

Without civic entrepreneurship, the public arena in many Arab Spring countries would crumble under the pressure of ongoing instability. This would be the true death knell of the region's revolutions, sending individuals back into the private sphere and placing the fate of these countries in the hands of the privileged few.